A Year of Walks:
Kent

Roy Woodcock

Published by Sigma Leisure – an imprint of
Sigma Press, 1 South Oak Lane, Wilmslow, Cheshire SK9 6AR, England.

British Library Cataloguing in Publication Data
A CIP record for this book is available from the British Library.

ISBN: 1-85058-655-1

Typesetting and Design by: Sigma Press, Wilmslow, Cheshire.

Cover photographs: clockwise, from top left – Lamberhurst church and golf course; Emmett's garden, near Westerham; Bedgebury; oast houses near Chartham
Sketches: Wendy Galassini
Cover design: MFP Design & Print
Photographs and maps: Roy Woodcock

Printed by: MFP Design and Print

Disclaimer: the information in this book is given in good faith and is believed to be correct at the time of publication. No responsibility is accepted by either the author or publisher for errors or omissions, or for any loss or injury howsoever caused. Only you can judge your own fitness, competence and experience.

Preface

This series of circular walks visits 12 of the outstanding locations in Kent and crosses delightful countryside in all of them. There are short cut and alternative options in many months and altogether there is a choice of over 20 walks. The walks are not rugged or arduous, but more for walkers seeking fresh air and exercise, whilst seeing the county of Kent in all its moods throughout the year. The choice of walks is inevitably personal: large areas in Kent are scenically attractive and appropriately known as the Garden of England. The county contains parts of two Areas of Outstanding Natural Beauty, the High Weald and Kent Downs.

The main walks are from 5 -16 miles in length and can be taken as a full day out, but most of them have short cuts or alternative options of 4-9 miles. This is to enable walkers to have a half day or more leisurely outing, or to suit families with small children. There are always features of interest on the walks, whether it is a nature reserve with flowers or birds, an old church or castle, the local geology, or historical links with large estates and magnificent houses. The world-famous White Cliffs of Dover have links with World War II and earlier battles, and nearby is the newest land in England, Samphire Hoe, created by using rock dug out during the construction of the Channel Tunnel.

It is hoped that references to the weather, the landscape and features of natural history which might be seen or experienced in each month will add to the pleasure, interest and enjoyment of each walk. The features of natural history mentioned are generally those which are likely to be seen during the walk, not the rare or shy for which a lengthy wait may be required. It is hoped that the walks will enable you to discover features of the landscape which perhaps had not been noticed before, and to appreciate the countryside as it changes through the year. Each month has its own particular attractions, but although the walks specifically refer to a particular month, they can all be enjoyed at any time of the year. The maps and the detailed description of the route will enable anyone to follow these walks without danger of getting lost, although local maps may be useful in providing further information about the areas which are being crossed. Any steep climbs are referred to in the description, as are any locations which might be available for refreshment.

The weather comments included with each month contain the general or average for that month but also a few specific to the year of 1998. Countryside comments are also both general to the month but also a few are relevant to the year of the walk, and the region described.

Advisory

Each walk is accompanied by a map and together with the detailed description of the walk should enable anyone to find and follow the route. However it will be useful to have the 1:25,000 Explorer or the 1:50,000 Landranger maps in case of problems with the route and also to provide information and detail about the surrounding area. It is always advisable to carry a compass, which can be especially useful in woodlands or in fog, when sense of direction may be lost.

Many places will be muddy, especially in winter, and some sections of the walks are steep or stony. Therefore, boots are advisable. It is also advisable, or even essential, to carry windproof and waterproof clothing, as well as a warm drink and some food if going out all day, even though there are locations for refreshment on most of the walks described.

Binoculars are very handy, especially if you are at all interested in bird life, and they sometimes help to pinpoint the location of stiles at the opposite side of a field. Cameras too are useful, as all the walks contain many photogenic locations.

All details were correct at the time of walking, mostly in 1998 or 99. All the walks follow public rights of way, and were free from obstructions at the time of last walking the routes described.

Contents

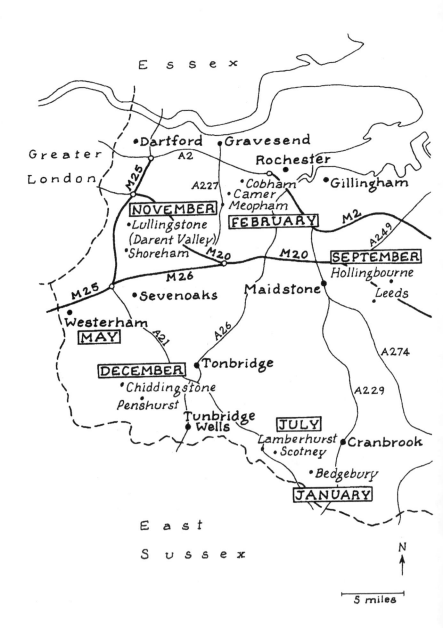

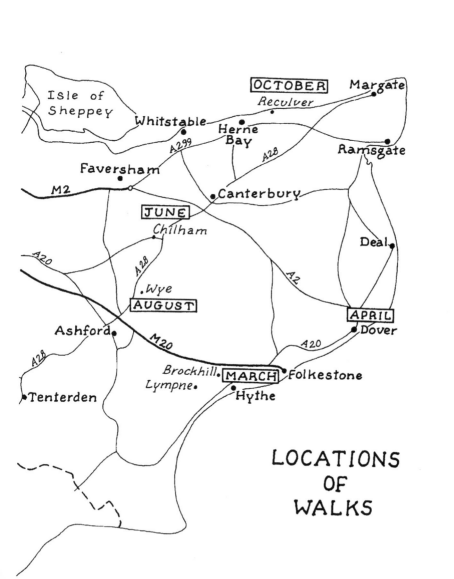

LOCATIONS
OF
WALKS

Introduction

Kent has a long east-west extent, stretching north of Sussex and south of London. The Sussex boundary extends from near Rye in a north-westerly direction towards Tonbridge and Sevenoaks, and then Surrey borders Kent one mile beyond Westerham. The county has a long coastline which is the boundary to the north and east.

The location in the south-east of England results in Kent being strongly influenced by proximity to the continent. Travel routes which pass through Kent are also influenced by its role as a residential and a commuting county as well as a tourist attraction with many holiday resorts along the coast. The total area is 373,063 hectares (11,441 sq.mls.) and the population is more than 1.5 million, making it one of the most populated counties in England, only exceeded by the larger municipal areas and by Essex and Hampshire. In spite of this high population, much of Kent is still very rural, and deserving of its name the Garden of England. It is so typical of a traditional type of English landscape, yet it is the first to receive travellers from Europe, whether invaders, refugees or tourists.

The geology of Kent is noted for its east-west orientation, with the dominating feature of the North Downs stretching from the western border to the coast at Folkestone, Dover and Deal. Sevenoaks, Maidstone and Ashford line the southern borders of the chalk, where the south facing steep slope or escarpment is prominent. North of the scarp, the chalk dip slope sinks gently to the north as far as Rochester, Faversham and Canterbury. The chalk dates from the Cretaceous geological period and was being formed 80-100 million years ago.

North of the chalk is the east-west area of the Thames lowlands, geologically young rocks (40-60 million years), mainly sands, clays and gravels of the Cainozoic era, although in the Margate and Ramsgate area the chalk outcrops again.

South of the chalk are east-west strips of clay and then sandstones from the Cretaceous period though older than the chalk, dating from 120-160 million years ago. These include the Gault clay which has been used for brick making in several locations, and gives rise to fairly rich though heavy soils. The sandstones on the other hand give rise to light and well-drained soils, which warm up quickly in the spring – useful for growing fruit or vegetables.

A large expanse of alluvium in the Romney-Dungeness area has been deposited by rivers and the sea, which have dumped large patches of shingle too, especially near the power station.

For anyone travelling either north to south, or south to north, these different areas of rocks will be passed in sequence, and many geologists visit Kent to see how the rock type influences the landscape. The youngest rocks are in the sands and clays in the north, and these form low and gentle scenery, with many marshy areas along the Thames estuary. The chalk creates its own characteristic scenery and in Kent there is a steep south facing slope and a gentle slope to the north. South of the chalk is the gault clay which creates low and often damp fields, and south of that the land rises to the harder sandstones, which create ridges of hills and are often infertile soils giving rise to areas of wood or heathland. Moving further south, the land undulates, with the higher ridges all being made of sandstone and the lower areas generally on clays.

The chalklands have been designated as the Kent Downs Area of Outstanding Natural Beauty, and this AONB covers 878 sq.kms. (339 sq.mls) and is a very precious area, being situated in the midst of a well-populated area and very close to London with its 6 million inhabitants. Also much of the North Downs land has been used for building towns and for the numerous roads which inevitably cross a well-populated area. Management of this area is very difficult with major conflicting views and needs. Part of the High Weald Area of Outstanding Natural Beauty is also in Kent, though part of this is in East Sussex. This AONB covers an area of 1450 sq.kms. (560 sq.mls.), stretching between Horsham, Tenterden and Rye. It is a region of fields, hedges, woodlands and some orchards, with sandstone ridges often being forest covered.

A famous long distance footpath, and now designated a National Trail, the North Downs Way extends the full length of this ridge of chalk, from Farnham in Surrey to Dover (there is also an extension going further west, as far as Winchester). At Boughton Lees the path divides, giving two alternatives as options, the northern branch passing through Canterbury on its way to Dover, and the southern branch going through Wye, Folkestone and thence to Dover.

Kent is well endowed with public footpaths, and they are mostly well marked and maintained. Numerous local walkers help to ensure that public rights of way have remained open, and many of the local councils have been actively involved in this work too.

As the climate warmed up after the Ice Age, differing types of vegetation gradually spread into this region, and most of the county became covered by scrub and woodland. By about 8000BC, birch and willow trees had become well established, and then Scots pine, hazel, oak and elm began to appear. Gradually alder and lime arrived too and then Britain became separated from the rest of Europe, and so changes slowed down. The area between the chalk of the North and South Downs is called The Weald, which takes its name from the Anglo-Saxon *wald* meaning wood.

As man moved in and settled, woodland was gradually cleared, especially in areas where settlement and farming were easier. This was often determined by the local geology, for example drier lands on chalk or sandstone. The geology also affected other occupations in addition to farming, as sandstone was used for building stone, clay was used for bricks, and an early iron industry was established in pre-Roman times. Local ironstone was smelted using charcoal made from the local forests, which also supplied oak for building ships.

Climatic changes of the past affected natural vegetation patterns, and so any modern-day climatic changes will only be part of the ongoing changes. Both at the present time and in former centuries, the British (and Kent) weather has been characterised by rapid changes. It is often said that the weather in Britain is so variable that all four seasons can be experienced in one day. Although this is too great a generalisation, there can certainly be rapid changes within a few hours, with the fast-moving Atlantic systems, which bring so much of our weather. Just because it is raining in the morning, does not mean it will not be a good day for walking.

Rain before seven, fine by eleven, is a well known weather saying, based on the idea that depressions are likely to pass over within about four hours.

Just as the weather keeps changing, although general patterns are similar, so too does the countryside keep changing through the seasons. The exact timings of plant growth and bird and butterfly breeding may vary slightly, but spring always comes, however cold and long the winter may be. Also it will rain again sometime, even if there is a prolonged dry spell in summer, and vice versa, the rainy spells do end sometime. The flowers grow, the crops are harvested, and the trees shed their leaves in the ongoing cycle of change. We sometimes forget what happened in the previous year or years, and are often surprised by the variability of the weather, however many times we have experienced similar conditions. If there is a cold spell in May we are surprised, and many journalists write about it as though it has never happened before – even though something similar happened twelve months previously. It may be that the hot, cold, wet and dry spells are more extreme at present possibly because of slight climatic changes caused by Global Warming. In much of 1997-98, climatic extremes were often blamed on El Niño, the ocean current off the coast of Peru. Whether this was correct and justified, only time will tell, perhaps when the next El Niño event occurs, in the year 2000, or 2001, or whenever?

January

Bedgebury

Mostly passing through woods which provide shelter if the weather is harsh, this walk is ideal for a wet or blowy day. A two-mile circuit round the Pinetum reveals a world wide selection of trees (Round the World in 80 minutes), and the extra miles in the surrounding woodlands will add to the enjoyment as well as providing an opportunity to see a variety of birds.

Distances: 5 miles, though several possible extensions are available if required with extra miles in the forest, a longer look round the Pinetum, or following the Forest Trail.

Time required: 2-3 hours for the basic walk, plus stopping time to look at trees or birds, plus any extensions added.

Terrain: undulating, but mostly along paths and well worn tracks, some of which can become very muddy.

Maps: Landranger 188 or Explorer 136.

Starting point: car park at GR 715337, which is reached along the B2079, to the north of Flimwell on the A21. Bus service from Tunbridge Wells to Hawkhurst.

Amenities: small snack bar in car park, or pub in Flimwell. Tourist Information Centres at Cranbrook (01580 712538) not open all year, or from the nearest large town of Royal Tunbridge Wells (01892 515675) — from where bus information is available.

The Month

Weather

The January average is some way between the two types of weather which affect us most years. Cold north or easterly weather generally balances spells of westerly mild conditions. When westerlies prevail, Kent is more sheltered than most parts of England, though the coastal strip is occasionally buffeted by strong winds. Northerly weather may affect the coastline along the Thames estuary to bring slight snowfalls, but the coldest weather is from the east, and this may hit Kent more severely than any other parts of the country. When temperatures in Germany fall to minus 10°C or lower, the winds from that direction warm up a little as they blow towards England, but may still give minus 2-3° to Kent. If the temperatures are lower the air tends to be dry and gives only slight snowfall. It is too cold for snow, as the old saying goes. But with temperatures of about zero, heavy snowfalls may hit Kent, especially the eastern part of the county. This snow tends to be dry and powdery. 1998 brought a below-average amount of easterly weather, and Kent like most of England was very mild for the first half of the month, though strong winds and some flooding affected coastal areas in the first week of the year. Daily maxima were about 8-12°C, though up to 14° for a couple of days. The second half of the month was much cooler, with northerly weather and temperatures only reaching 3-4°, but this period was much drier. Light snow fell on the North Downs on the 25th. One of the worst years in recent decades was 1940 when heavy snowfalls and ice storms paralysed much of south-east England.

"The blackest month of all the year, is the month of Janiveer" can certainly be true in some years, but February is often a worse month in terms of cold and snow, though not in length of daylight.

The Countryside

Mild Januarys enable the summer crops to be growing slightly, though many fields have not yet been planted, because of the danger of severe frosts. A sharp frost is sometimes considered to be good for a ploughed field as it breaks up large lumps and also kills off a few of the insect pests. A ploughed field may also be good for rooks, jackdaws, pigeons and gulls which search for food, and also for smaller birds, the larks and finches, especially if any stubble remains. Cold weather in Europe will cause large numbers of birds to migrate in the search for food, and Kent is often their first stopping point. Common birds such as starlings, come in huge numbers and Scandinavian thrushes, the redwings and fieldfares also appear. Around the shores on the mud flats and coastal marshes, large numbers of ducks, geese and waders come for the rich pickings renewed at every high tide. The deciduous trees are bare at this time of year, but the appearance of the bark is often a way in which some trees can be identified, and the bare branches with their glorious silhouettes against a blue sky can be one of the joys of winter walking. A few red berries may have survived from the autumn, and the lambs tails catkins

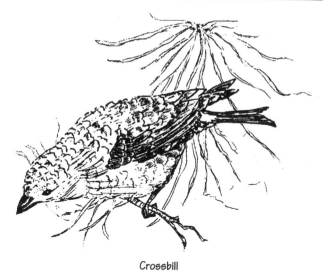

Crossbill

will be hanging down on the hazel trees. Bedgebury is a particularly good location to see birds in winter, as many visitors call in here. The more open state of the woodlands is a help, and tits, goldcrests, woodpeckers are always here, and hawfinches and crossbills can often be seen.

Along the Way

Bedgebury Pinetum

The Pinetum was established in 1923, and planting started in 1925. It covers an area of 300 acres (120 hectares), is home to the National collection of conifers and claims to be the finest collection of coniferous trees anywhere in the world. It contains trees from all over the world, including USA, Japan, Scotland, New Zealand, Morocco and the Himalayas. The collection is used both to conserve species and to try out new species in British conditions. The Pinetum is open all year, from 10am until 7pm, or until dusk in the winter, and there is an admission charge. The Information Centre is open daily from 10am until 5pm from March until Christmas, but only at weekends 10-4 during January and February. Pinetum Pantry is open for refreshments on similar dates. (Phone is 01580 211044). The trees in the Pinetum are mostly conifers, and the same is also true in the

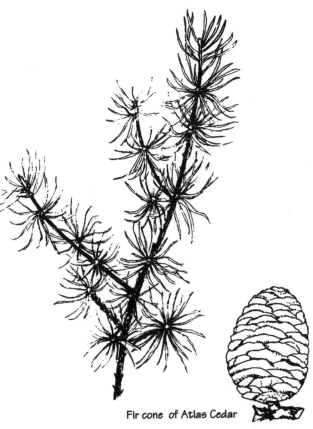

Fir cone of Atlas Cedar

Bedgebury Forest but here there are stands of sweet chestnut and many other broad-leaved deciduous trees. The Pinetum was founded by Kew, but was taken over by the Forestry Commission in 1961, and immediately made plans for opening to the public. The Mansion adjacent to the Pinetum was the home of the Beresford Hope family, but is now a girls' school. The Pinetum is attractive and interesting at any time of the year, and if snow-covered can certainly be described as a winter wonderland. Seasonal attractions include spring flowers, then rhododendrons and azaleas in May, and the autumn colours of the conifers now added to by the recent planting of trees and shrubs particularly noted for their autumn colours. Autumn is also interesting for the large number of fungi which grow in the Pinetum.

Bedgebury Forest

This ancient forest has existed from pre-Saxon times, and has grown on a mixture of sands and clays of the Hastings Beds, a sub division of the Wealden rocks of the Cretaceous period. Considerable variations in soil type and water-holding capacity have helped to create a variety of woodland types. These variations have become part of the

Forestry Authority policy to create a range of differing habitats for wild life. The woods contain some open areas, as well as planting of various ages, and a variety of trees, including some deciduous. Hawfinches and crossbills are special winter birds, but there are also bramblings and siskins, as well as resident tawny owls and sparrowhawks. Nesting birds include tree creeper, nuthatch, woodcock (a very important bird), stock dove, a few pairs of nightingales and most famous of all are the nightjars.

Forest Trail

This trail extends for about two miles through the numerous plots of land where many different trees are planted to compare rates of growth. Many of the plots were damaged or destroyed in the October 1987 storm, but the variety of trees can still be seen, and 21 information posts

Sunlight through the trees in Bedgebury Forest

will explain some of what can be seen. A free coloured map is available from the Information Centre to show the plan of the Pinetum and also the route of this trail.

The Walk

From the entrance to the Pinetum (1), go straight along the surfaced path, and as it begins to descend and divides, take the left turn down into the valley. Already a variety of coniferous trees will have come into view. Keep to the left of the pond, with a tall cypress and a pine across on the other side, and as we bend right round the end of the pond, pass a huge sequoia on our right. Continue along the surfaced path, with the cypress swamp and then Marshall Lake on our left. This lake was created in the mid-19th century as part of the Bedgebury House parkland. Water lilies and probably some ducks and geese can be seen on this lake. Many small land birds are also likely to be seen and heard in this area. Seats and picnic tables are located around here if required. Pass the rhododendrons on the right, and then a wooden footbridge across the lake to the left. Bend left at

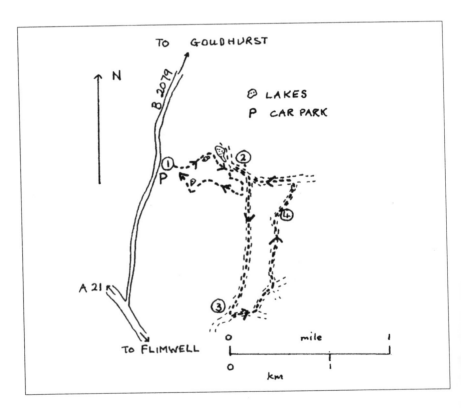

the end of the lake, to reach a T-junction of paths, where we turn right, along a broad surfaced path.

After a few metres, go left through a small gate and climb across the Dwarf and Slow Growing conifer collection, to a gate at the top of this small fenced area. Once through this gate, turn left, and follow the narrow stony path beyond the signs to the toilets to reach another small gate, beyond which is a broad driveway. Go out on to this driveway and turn right (2).

As we proceed along the drive, notice the Forest Trail on the left, and then the buildings of the Forestry Department. Just beyond the house on our right, the track goes straight ahead and we shall return along it in an hour or so, but for the walk through the forest, we begin by turning right along a bridleway to walk south through the woodlands. Just over the holly hedge on the right is the Pinetum.

Follow the broad track, and soon pass a major track going off sharply back to the right, but we keep straight ahead. We are now in the Bedgebury Forest, with conifers to the right but many deciduous trees to the left. Ignore the track which turns left, and after a few more metres ignore the track which goes off diagonally to the right, at an old brick water tank. Still following the blue arrow for bridleway, go slightly uphill, with conifers now on our left. At the next junction of tracks head slightly right, which is really still straight on. Notice that bracken is a common undergrowth in this area. At the next major junction the signed bridleway bends right, but we turn sharp left here (3), along a broad stony track (bearing 80-90 degrees) with a lot of sweet chestnut on the left.

Turn left at the first junction, just before the point where the straight-ahead route can be seen beginning to climb. The bearing along the grassy track is about 40, and we begin to descend slightly. Reach a cross tracks, were we turn left, going slightly uphill on a bearing of about 340, between sweet chestnut on both sides. At the top of a slight climb, reach a cross tracks and go straight ahead for 40m, and soon reach a diagonal gravelled track on which we turn right, on a bearing of about 20. Continue along this major track, between young planting on both sides, and ignore the broad track going off to the right. Just keep straight on and descend slightly before reaching a junction of five tracks (4). Keep ahead, slightly to the right of straight on, but still following the main stony track. There may be little sissing noises in the trees all around, as birds are likely to be busy searching for food, especially the tits and goldcrests, but the noise of robins and wrens may also be heard, as well as the bigger jays, and woodpeckers, both green and great spotted.

Reach a simple iron barrier gate at the end of this track, and just beyond here, at a major T-junction, turn left (bearing about 270). This is a lovely stretch of mixed woodland, and after about a quarter mile, we reach the point where the track we began our walk into the forest goes off to the left. We keep straight on between the buildings, to reach the small gate (2) which leads us back into the Pinetum.

Re-enter the Pinetum though the small gate and follow the narrow path, with the Dwarf and Slow growing conifer collection on our right. Pass beneath the massive Crimean pine (pinus nigra), with a name tag on it, as have so many of the trees – fortunately. Go slightly downhill, and at the bottom when the path divides, turn left along a narrow though surfaced path to reach a rock garden on the left and an old brick building on the right, formerly the Visitors Centre, School room and Information Area, with small wooden seats and tables. Just beyond the building the narrow stony path ends, but keep straight ahead, across an open area, over a small stream and then climb up through the trees. As the path levels off, turn right to reach the wire fence surrounding the Glory Hole Garden. Bear left along the margin of this sunken area, the former rubbish dump for Bedgebury House in Victorian times, with the holly hedge to the left, marking the edge of the Pinetum and just beyond this is the track along which we walked in the early part of the walk. Pass beneath the graceful Mexican white pines with their fine needles.

Reach the wide grassy pathway called Hill's Avenue, which extends down to the right, which is the way we turn, to pass across the middle of the Pinetum. The view along the grassy way is one of many magnificent views seen – and these colossal giants of nature do make humans seem small and insignificant. Walk along Hill's Avenue and after about 50 metres turn left into the newest part of the Pinetum, to walk into an area of cypress trees, to reach post number 24, where the path splits. Fork right slightly to reach post 22, then on to 21, and then turn right to descend to the stream, and post number 20. These numbers can all be seen on the pamphlet "Trees of the World".

Cross the stream, and after 20 metres reach the broad footpath known as Lady Mildred's Drive, once the main drive from Bedgebury House out to the London Road, and turn right to walk parallel to the stream. Reach Hill's Avenue again, and to the right notice the small pond, tiny waterfall, a bridge and steps, but our way ahead is to the left. Before doing so, go straight ahead for a further 20-30m to visit the Old Man of Kent, a giant silver fir (*abies grandis*), the tallest tree in Kent (about 50 metres), and the oldest tree in the Pinetum, dating from about 1840. It is tree No. 8 on the Round the World guide pamphlet, and No. 34 in Trees of the World.

Retrace steps to Hill's Avenue and walk on up the slope, to come on to a surfaced path again. Western hemlock and Douglas fir are close together; as they would be in their native Oregon USA. Go over the top and then downhill to walk round the left end of the lake and through the redwood grove, where many of the trees were planted in 1925. Climb up the other side of the valley, passing the oriental sweet gum (liquidambar orientalis) noted for their autumn colours, and the Paper bark birch trees, to return to the starting point

As we leave the Pinetum, we pass the notice saying that these fine trees are a scientific collection of national importance planted to create a landscape of interest and beauty. It certainly succeeds.

February

Camer, Meopham, Cobham

The main walk undulates through woodland and across farmland, on clearly marked footpaths, visiting Meopham, Havel, Luddesdown and Cobham on the way. Even in the 19th century, Londoners enjoyed getting out of the city into the countryside, and this walk passes through an area popular with Charles Dickens. With a good starting point in one of Kent's splendid Country Parks, this circuit may test your powers of pronunciation, visiting Camer (often pronounced Kammer) and Meopham (pronounced Meppem).

Distance: main walk, 11 miles with a short cut of 7 miles, and shorter circuit of 5 miles.

Time required: about 5 hours, 3 hours or 2 hours respectively.

Terrain: fairly gentle, with a couple of steep climbs, but nothing too strenuous, although there are several stretches likely to be muddy. Stiles are quite numerous.

Maps: O.S. Landranger 177 or Explorer 163.

Starting point: car park at Camer, GR 649669 (ample parking space, and toilets). This can be reached from Meopham along the A227, then on the B2009 and take the first turn on the right. Buses from Gravesend to Sevenoaks run through Meopham, and frequent trains run to Sole Street, which is very close to the route.

Amenities: Meopham is the nearest town; refreshments are available here and also at pubs in Harvel, Lower Luddesdown and Cobham. **Nearest TIC** is at Gravesend (01474 337600).

The Month

Weather

Generally a cold month, often the coldest of the year in Kent, when easterly winds from the high pressure over Europe and Siberia send icy weather across Europe into England. In this easterly weather, although the temperatures of minus 10°C. or minus 20° in Europe warm up as they travel westwards, temperatures in Kent are often below zero and light snowfalls occur. Any snow tends to be light and dusty, because of low temperatures, and can be easily blown into drifts, creating chaos on roads and railway. In some years, including 1998, the easterly weather is kept out by westerly air. Temperatures were much warmer than the February average daily maxima of about 6°C. There were frosts for a couple of days at the beginning of the month and then mild weather really began, with daily maxima of 10°-15°, and up to 16° and 17° on one occasion – brought by southerly tropical air from the Azores. Many of these mild days were sunny too, and there are likely to be many days in June or July which will have less pleasant conditions. The last week of the month was cooler, and northerly arctic air brought some frosty weather, but even so the month was one of the warmest ever recorded, with the same temperature average as in 1990, and the only warmer Februarys ever recorded were in 1779 and 1869. At the opposite end of records for the past, were 1795 and 1814, when February saw frost fairs on the Thames, and in more recent times there was ice upstream from Hampton in February 1963.

The Countryside

The very mild weather encouraged many birds to start singing earlier than usual, as they began to work on their territorial claims. Also many of the spring flowers grew, with daffodils and primroses appearing by mid-month, often growing alongside the snowdrops

Orchard in winter

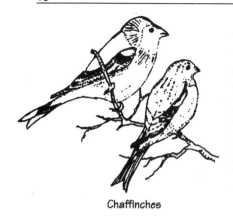

Chaffinches

which were still numerous. Although the winter visiting birds were still around, many of the residents were showing early signs of summer. Ducks on the lakes were in summer plumage and were often to be seen in pairs, and in the gardens and hedgerows, chaffinches were in their brighter summer plumage, and blackbirds and thrushes were showing signs of pairing. In tree tops, the rooks were busy at their nests, offering sticks to mates, or fighting rivals over the best sticks available for nest buildings. Molehills were numerous in gardens and fields, an indication that the ground was softening and worms were moving back up towards the surface – and so the moles were following them. Also, in the fields, lambs were appearing – adding a new sight and sound to the countryside. In the woods, early greenery including cuckoopint leaves, was showing on the ground, in the midst of the brown of last year's leaves. Woodland areas were also brown with bracken, though during the frequent sunny spells, this was looking almost golden in colour. Crops were growing in the farm fields, and grass too was beginning to shoot up. Many farmers were busy muck spreading, adding a rich aroma to the fresh air experienced whilst walking.

St Mathias Day (24th February) has the old saying: *"The St Mathee sends the sap up the trees"* – implying that this is the day on which the trees begin to stir, and this would certainly be true for many trees this year. Other sayings for St Mathias are less encouraging and optimistic. For example, *"If it freezes on St Mathias' Day, it will freeze for a month"*.

Along the Way

Meopham

The village green is claimed as the site of the first recorded cricket match, in 1778, between the local team and Cobham. Alongside the green are two pubs, one of which is called The Cricketers and contains a collection of cricket memorabilia. Just along the road from The Cricketers is the Meopham windmill, built by the Killick Brothers in 1801, on the site of an earlier mill. It is a smock mill, in which the main part of the mill, the smock, is stationary (or fixed), and the upper part or cap rotates. The mill is a working mill and museum, but is only open to visitors from June to September, on Sunday and Bank Holiday afternoons. The ground floor of the mill is used by the Parish Council. The village church is St John the Baptist, and dates from 1325, having been built on the

Near Meopham Green

site of an old Saxon church. An unusual item of its history, is that it was damaged by an earthquake in 1382.

Camer Country Park

This covers an area of nearly 19 hectares (46 acres), with some open parkland, woodlands and grassy areas, as well as a playground and picnic areas. It is now owned and managed by Gravesham Borough Council, and is open throughout the year.

St Peter and St Paul Luddesdown

A church on this site was mentioned in the Domesday Book, and a Norman tower still survives. Originally a 13th and 14th-century church, extensive restoration work was completed in 1866, and the wall paintings date from 1894. Roman tiles have been included in the stonework of this tower. Nearby is the old two-storied Manor House, Luddesdown Court, an L-shaped building of flint and Caen stone, and a Grade I Listed building. Thought to date from the 13th century or earlier, it is reputed to be the oldest continuously occupied house in England. It contains medieval wall paintings and a minstrels' gallery.

Cobham

This ancient village has many interesting old buildings using a variety of building materials, stone, flint, hung tiles and weatherboards. Outstanding is the 13th-century church of St Mary Magdalene, containing one of the world's finest collections of medieval brasses, with a total of 19, of which 11 are complete. They date from 1298-1529. Fifteen of the brasses form a pavement in the chancel, and beyond these is the alabaster and black marble tomb of George Brooke, Earl of Cobham and his wife Anne Bray, dating from 1561. The village has had many links with the Cobham family, and also had links with Charles Dickens. The Leather Bottle opposite the church dates from 1629, and was a Royalist meeting place in the Civil War. It was often visited by Dickens, who described it as "a clean and commodious village ale house". He featured the pub in "The Pickwick Papers", and it is where Mr. Tupman drowned his sorrows after being jilted by Rachel Wardle.

Mr Pickwick is on the sign of The Leather Bottle in Cobham

Alongside the church is the

flint-faced Stone House, built in the 14th century as a home for the priests, and later used to accommodate travellers. Behind the church is Cobham College, which dates from 1362 – founded by Sir John de Cobham. It was a college for priests, then became alms-houses for people living in the parish, and is now used as sheltered accommodation. It is a haven of peace, with its courtyard resembling an Oxford College. Known to Dickens, these almshouses were probably the basis of Titbull's Almshouses in "The Uncommercial Traveller".

Further along the village street is Owletts, a 17th-century red brick house built for Bonham Hayes in 1684, formerly the home of the architect Sir Herbert Baker, and now owned by the National Trust but only open from April to September. Opposite Owletts is a renovated store barn on staddle stones, behind which is a modernised group of luxury residences. The village pump is alongside the road, and is classed as a listed building.

The Walk

Leave the Country Park (1) and walk along the road heading south for about 200 metres then go diagonally right across a field. Walk on through a small wood and across the next field to reach a road and houses on the edge of Meopham. Cross straight over the road and walk along Whitehill Road. Beyond the houses and at the bottom of the hill, go right over a stile, and up the hill to another stile, then alongside the hedge to another stile and out on to a track. Beyond a kissing gate, we pass the Old Oast House dated 1840 on our right, and emerge on the busy main road near Meopham Green (2). At the edge of the Green, note the old water fountain, a memorial to the Coronation of King Edward and Queen Alexandra, dated August 9th 1902.

Adjacent to the Green are The Cricketers Inn and the windmill, but our walk goes on from the far corner of the Green beyond the pavilion and the location of the cricket nets – signposted "bridleway". Take the track going downhill, and ignore the left fork, keeping straight ahead to emerge in an open field at the bottom of Happy Valley. Walk on towards the woods in the distance, but fork left before reaching them, to go up to the top corner of the field. Turn left along

Heron Hill Lane, a sunken track going uphill through the woods, and at the top where the track bends left, go right and into a field. Follow the path past the first telegraph pole and across the middle of the field. Go over a stile and along the hedge, out to the road in Harvel. Turn left, then right at the Amazon and Tiger, pass the Post Office and turn left at the duck pond and the small green, on to Dean Lane (3).

Leave the village along Dean Lane, and after about 200 metres go left over a stile and up to the corner of the field. Go on over the stile and walk in a narrow line of trees, keeping straight ahead to the bottom of a dry valley. Go right, over a stile, and follow the edge of a wood, bending round to the left. Turn left at the end of the wood, and cross two fields and a patch of scrubby woodland, to emerge at a narrow road. Go straight across and up the hill, but where the track bends left, we turn right, to follow the narrow path (number 227) for a mile in scrubby woodland, rich in bird life and the early signs of spring flowers.

At a major cross-paths (GR 661656) with a notice about walks from Camer (4), go straight ahead over the stile and fork left (224) across the field. Go downhill and then up the next field to a minor road. Cross straight over following signs to Sole Street and Henley Street, and after two small fields enter Henley Wood, an old woodland with ancient banks and ditches which were probably marking estate boundaries. Emerge from the wood to walk along its margin, and when this path turns left, still following the edge of the woods, is the point of decision (5). The path now joins the Wealdway, coming across from left to right. This long distance route extends for 80 miles through Sussex and Kent, from Gravesend to Beachy Head.

Short cut

For the short route back to Camer, turn left here (242) following the margin of the woods, and following the Wealdway. At the end of the wood, keep straight ahead along the track, passing a modern brick building adjacent to an old house with hung tiles. Pass a bridleway going right and then after a few trees reach the point where a path comes in from the left, and two come in from the right (6). The path which comes across the field to our right, passing to the right of a pylon is the route of the **main walk**, and the short circular walk from Cobham.

Keep straight ahead, and when the track bends sharp right, turn left at a stile and a gap in the fence, into the Camer Country Park, following the yellow arrows. Pass through a small copse, and a few more trees, to reach the main grassland area of the park. Head straight across the middle of the open ground with scattered trees, in a south-westerly direction, passing the children's playground and return to the car park starting point.

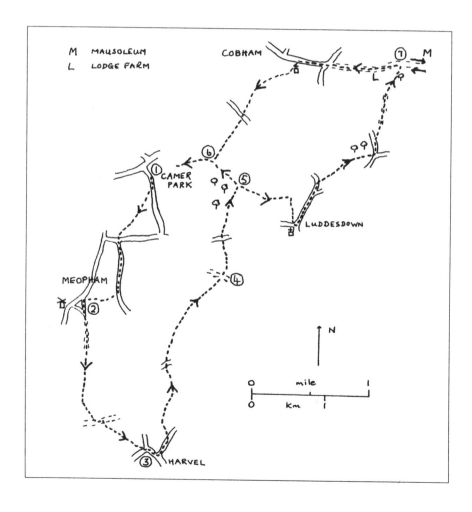

Main walk, continued

We turn right on the Wealdway (225) with a hedge on the left. Pass through a small wood and turn right to go downhill to a stile and a few bushes. Turn left along a horizontal path and shortly reach another stile. Keep straight ahead until the church is to the right, in the trees below. Turn right (188) to descend the slope, passing to the right of the cricket pitch and Luddesdown village hall, to emerge on a minor road. The village hall was formerly a school, built in 1865.

Our route ahead is to the left, following this road, but before continuing, detour to the church of St Peter and St Paul. Its neighbour is another impressive building, Luddesdown Court, which has a large open thatched barn, used as a garage. From the church, follow the little road, as far as Lower Luddesdown. At the Golden Lion fork left along Henley Street, signposted to Cobham and Gravesend, and passing Darnley Cottage. Walk uphill, and where the road bends left, fork right along a path (226) leading across a large open field, beneath three lines of pylons. At the end of three fields, go over the stile and turn right, to walk through the edge of Cobhambury Wood, a very varied mixed wood, rich in bird life. Emerge on to a minor road, at a road junction.

Turn left along the road and over to the right is a wood called Shoulder of Mutton Shaw, a shaw being the old name for a small patch of woodland between two fields. After 200 metres, fork right along a stony track, and pass beneath the main railway line. Either follow the track up to Lodge Farm, or just after reaching the corner of the woods of Cobham Park, fork right through sweet chestnut trees, along a path which follows the line of the telegraph poles up the hill. At the top, emerge on to a flat grassy area and go straight ahead for a few metres (7).

At the grassy track, turn left for Lodge Farm and Cobham, though if you wish to visit the Cobham Mausoleum, turn right for about three-quarters of a mile. The Mausoleum is a Portland stone building, designed by Wyatt in 1783 and intended to be the burial place of the Earls of Darnley, though never used. Near to the Mausoleum is the Toe Monument, where the 5th Earl of Darnley cut off his own toe, when demonstrating how to use an axe.

Our onward route is to the left, along the track, headings westwards, and Cobham Hall can be seen to the north, away to our right. The Hall is an Elizabethan red brick house, dating from 1584, and was the ancestral home of the Cobhams, Brookes and Darnleys. It is set in 60 hectares (150 acres) of parkland, designed by Humphry Repton for the 4th Earl of Darnley. Dickens used to love walking here, and, as a friend of Lord Darnley he was given a key to the park, and could ramble there whenever he wished. W.G. Grace played cricket here in the park, but it is now an Independent girls school. The gardens are being restored by the Cobham Hall Heritage Trust, and both the gardens and surrounding woodlands are a mass of colour in the spring.

Follow the driveway leading out of Cobham Park, passing Lodge Farm with its old dovecot. Reach the B2009 where the avenue of lime trees comes from Cobham Hall. These trees were planted in 1987, to replace the former limes which were badly damaged in the severe gale (called the hurricane) of that year. Walk into the village of Cobham, passing the war memorial; the Ship Inn, possibly built from the timbers of a ship that went aground off Sheerness; the flint school dated 1874; the Village shop; the Darnley Arms (possibly dating from the 12th century); the Leather Bottle; and the church. Near the end of the village is the pump, now a scheduled monument, and beyond that is Owletts. Our onward route is on the path past the west end of the church.

Pass the College, walk on the surfaced path between holly bushes, and turn sharp right at the end of this path, just before the modern gravestones. Go through the kissing gate and fork left slightly on footpath NS187, a well-worn route towards a group of three pylons, passing through an enormous orchard. At the end of this orchard bend slightly left, follow a windbreak of pollarded poplars sheltering a pear orchard, and reach a kissing gate and a road.

Cross over the road, pass the stile, through a small field (soft fruit in 1998) and over the railway on the footbridge. The path leads into the next field, and after about 100 metres reaches a cross-paths, and keep straight ahead to the end of the field, where we join the route used for the short cut on the Wealdway (6), and turn right along the track.

Shorter options

For a 7-mile walk starting from Camer, follow the main walk and the short-cut route described above.

For a 5-mile walk starting from Cobham, begin at the village school (GR672685) where there is a parking area adjacent to the playing fields. Walk along the village street to the Leather Bottle, and turn left to pass the church and the old College, following the route of the main walk. On reaching the Wealdway at point number 6, turn left along the track to point 5. Keep straight ahead here and follow the instructions for the main walk, passing through Luddesdown, Lower Luddesdown and Cobham Park on the circuit back to the delightful village of Cobham.

March

Brockhill and Lympne

Differing types of Kent countryside can be seen at their best on this walk, which visits woodland, streams, a canal and farmland, with occasional views of the sea and Romney Marsh. The walk takes in many aspects of history, with Roman ruins, a castle, and relics of Napoleonic wartime as well as a Country Park and the urban development of Hythe.

Distances: 7½ miles, with a shorter alternative of 6 miles (starting at Lympne church GR 119347).

Time required: 3-4 hours or 2-3 hours for the alternative.

Terrain: mostly gentle though can be muddy in places

Maps: Explorer 138 and Landranger 189.

Starting point: GR 148359, which can be reached by leaving the M20 at junction 11, and turning left along the A20 towards Folkestone for less than half a mile and then turning right along a minor road which passes Sandling station before reaching Brockhill Country Park.

Amenities: Nearest town is Hythe, with good bus links, a choice of pubs and restaurants. There is also a TIC (01303 267799)

The Month

Weather

March is a month of many changes, and normally will experience signs of all four seasons sometime during the month, with milder southerly or westerly weather alternating with cool easterly or northerly spells.

"The spring she is a young maid, she does not know her mind" is a rather poetic way of emphasising the changeable nature of the month.

In 1998, March proved to be the one of the mildest on record, though not as mild as March 1997. The first and last weeks were un-settled, with frequent falls of rain (and snow in Scotland), and high pressure dominated during the second and third weeks, with good spells of sunshine. Mild weather saw temperatures rise to 14° or 15°C. on several days, and there were night minima of 10° and 11° near the end of the month, comparable to average figures for June. These were due to powerful flows of air from the south, which even brought Saharan dust as far north as England.

The old saying, *"In March much snow, To plants and trees much woe"* was hardly relevant in 1998.

March 20 was the official first day of spring, though meteorologists always regard the 1st March as the beginning of spring, for reasons of convenience rather than belief in its reliability. All parts of the world receive equal daylight at the time of the spring equinox, and certainly the extra daylight is becoming apparent by the end of the month.

The Countryside

The first signs of spring are generally evident during the month, but this year they were more numerous and earlier than usual. The old

Wood anemone

saying that *"It is not spring until you can put a foot down on twelve daisies"* was not really required as there were many pieces of evidence. Common birds including great tits and song thrushes were singing noisily, especially on sunny days. A few skylarks were heard and before the end of the month the repetitive call of the chiffchaffs, the first of our summer visitors were ringing out from the bare trees, where the first small green leaves were opening. Pussy willows were showing their delicate colours and many hedges were beginning to show some green. Many farm fields were also green with winter crops which had begun to grow taller, yet other farm fields were pristine brown, having just been ploughed in preparation for spring sowing. Farm tractors were often followed by birds, more gulls than rooks which is an increasingly common sight, as increasing numbers of gulls seem to live inland. Views over Romney Marsh revealed many ploughed fields and crops already growing well – rape was particularly advanced. Flowers added colour along hedges and field margins, and the last of the snowdrops had hardly disappeared before the primroses, violets, wood anemones and celandines had grown. Before the end of the month the first bluebells had appeared too, and the first blackthorn bushes were in flower. Frog spawn could be seen in many of the ponds and streams, and even in small puddles which will dry up, as frogs, unlike toads, are not very selective in where they leave their eggs.

Along the Way

Lympne

Pronounced Lim, this village is said to be 'a word you cannot pronounce if you see it, or spell if you hear it'. It takes its name from the River Liman which used to flow across Romney Marsh from west to east to just below the castle. Here was a lagoon, which silted up when the river broke through after huge storms. The Roman port built here in the third century was called Portus Lemanis.

The ragstone castle is perched on top of what appears to be an escarpment, but is an inland cliff, the former coastline, with wonderful views across Romney Marsh. Built originally in the 14th century, the castle is really a fortified manor house and its outstanding features include the panelled Great Hall, and the turret stairways to the tops of the towers, from where France is clearly visible. Archbishop Lanfranc (1070-1089) granted the castle in perpetuity to the Archdeacons of Canterbury. It passed into private ownership in 1870, and was extensively restored in 1908. It is a private house and not open to the public at present.

Next door to the castle, also built of ragstone, is the parish church

Lympne Castle

of St Stephen, reached through a large lych-gate near which are the mounting steps for horseborne church goers. Originally a Norman church with 13th-century additions, parts of the tower date from the 11th century, and the porch and doorway into the aisle are 14th century. Much of the church has been built of local ragstone. Some windows were destroyed by a flying bomb in 1944, and the roof was damaged.

There has long been a small airport at Lympne, though it has been called Ashford airport since 1969. Regular services hop over to France and it was a very important airfield in the days of pioneer flying, when many experimental flights took place from here.

Port Lympne

The animal park is one of two founded by John Aspinall (the other being Howletts), and extends over an area of 140 hectares (350 acres), and contains elephants, tigers and many other animals. A trailer ride provides an easy way of seeing the park. Also in the park are an historic mansion, beautiful landscaped gardens and many children's activities.

Brockhill Country Park

The estate was bought by Kent County Council in 1947, and the Country Park was opened in 1986. The Brockhill Estate has existed since Norman times, and the old manor house is said to have been haunted. The Park extends over 22 hectares (54 acres) and is open daily from 9am until dusk. It contains a lake, woodlands, numerous footpaths and barbecue and picnic area, and a small snack bar. The varied bird life which may be seen or heard includes three types of woodpeckers (the great spotted may be heard drumming), tree creepers, nuthatches, little owls and tawny owls, warblers, tits, as well as kestrels and sparrow hawks. Ducks and moorhens live on the lake. There is also a wealth of flowers and trees, with an important wetland area. Plant life is becoming prolific by the end of March, with many flowers and greenery.

Hythe

One of the original five Cinque Ports, which had to provide ships for the king, whenever required, Hythe remained an important port until the silting of the Leman estuary in the 14th century. The town declined following the silting, but has revived more recently for holidays and retirement. The name Hythe means a haven or landing place. Fears of invasion at the time of Napoleon led to the construction of the Royal Military Canal and several Martello towers. A total of 74 Martello towers were built along the Sussex and Kent coasts, although only 26 remain. They were named after Cape Martella in Corsica where a British attack in 1794 was successfully overcome. The church of St Leonard stands up on the hillside and rather unusually, the chancel is 13 steps up from the Norman nave, built this way because of lack of space. It originates from the late 12th century, but was rebuilt in the 13th century and many changes came in later centuries too. In the churchyard is a memorial to Lionel Lukin (1742-1834) who invented the lifeboat. Half a mile to the north of Hythe is Saltwood castle, originally a Norman castle but now a private house. It was from here that four knights rode to Canterbury to kill Thomas à Becket, in 1170.

Royal Military Canal

The canal was constructed by Sir John Moore, and dug as part of the coastal defences in the Napoleonic Wars. It runs along the foot of the inland cliff, and almost turns Romney into an island. There are bends on the canal, every one third of a mile, to serve as locations for guns facing along the canal to intercept any invaders. When Hitler threatened in 1940-41, the Royal Military Canal was refortified with concrete pill boxes. It is now a Scheduled Ancient Monument. The canal is 28 miles in length, from Hythe to Pett Level, is 2.7 metres (9ft) deep and 18 metres (60ft) wide, and was built between 1804 and 1809. It was last used commercially in 1907, but is now an important routeway for walkers. In addition, it helps to drain a wet low-lying area.

Symbol of the Saxon
Shore Way

The Saxon Shore Way, which follows the canal for several miles, is Kent's longest long distance footpath, extending for 140 miles. It mostly follows the coastline, but we see it going a little way inland. The Way is signed by a logo of a red winged helmet.

Romney, Hythe and Dymchurch Light Railway

The railway has rolling stock, one-third normal size, and its construction was inspired by Captain J.E.P. Howey. There are ten engines and seventy-five passenger coaches on the line, which opened in 1927. It runs fourteen miles from Dungeness Lighthouse to Hythe, and is the world's smallest public railway line. The gauge is of 15" (38cm).

Romney Marsh

This area has been formed by changing sea levels during the last 10,000 years, and by sea and river deposition during recent centuries. A few hundred years ago, Rye, Winchelsea and Lympne were on the coast, and floods and storms brought in deposits which gradually built up, though could change frequently and rapidly. Now the marsh is protected by sea walls and is crossed by numerous drainage ditches, to create the flat grazing land to be seen today. Sheep are numerous, and Romney is also home to a large selection of interesting plants and birds.

The Walk

Walk from the noticeboards near the visitor centre (1), following signs to the lake. Go down the hill, through the barbecue and picnic area to the lake. Cross a tiny stream and enter the woods, rich in flowers and bird life. Moorhens, coots and ducks live on the lake. The path leads alongside the right side of the lake, where a major restoration project has been taking place, because of the deterioration of the water quality. Large fish species have been moved to allow aquatic plants to develop, as too many have been uprooted by large numbers of fish foraging for food. Smaller fish have also been removed to enable the zooplankton such as daphnia to graze on the phytoplankton and algae which occur in the lake in summer.

Continue along the right side of the stream, ignoring the small bridge and then a larger bridge crossing over the stream. Keep straight ahead, with a field on the right, in which there may be sheep. The sheep, with their lambs, will be adding to the local noises, and occasionally the hoot of the train on Romney can be heard.

We reach the boundary of the Brockhill Country Park (2) and go over a stile (note the path coming in from the right – the route of the shorter alternative) then cross the wooden bridge to the other side of the stream – which is broader and quite rocky here. Follow the path through the trees, though an open field can be seen to the left. After a short climb, and just before reaching the houses, the path splits and we fork right, to stay in the trees, with the stream down to our right. Emerge to an open patch of grass, with a small playground area and a Land Drainage Structure behind a wire fence. Pass this fence and keep ahead along the road (Turnpike Hill), between modern houses, to reach the main road.

Turn left, and follow the road down towards the bridge over the canal. Although our route ahead is on the near (north) side of the canal, it may be worth crossing the bridge to visit the cafe or look at the station on the R, H and D railway line.

Cross back over the canal bridge and turn along Green Lane, which is signposted Saxon Shore Way, and after a few metres we can get on to the embankment of the Royal Military Canal. We can stride out for the gentle, flat two and a half miles as we follow the canal,

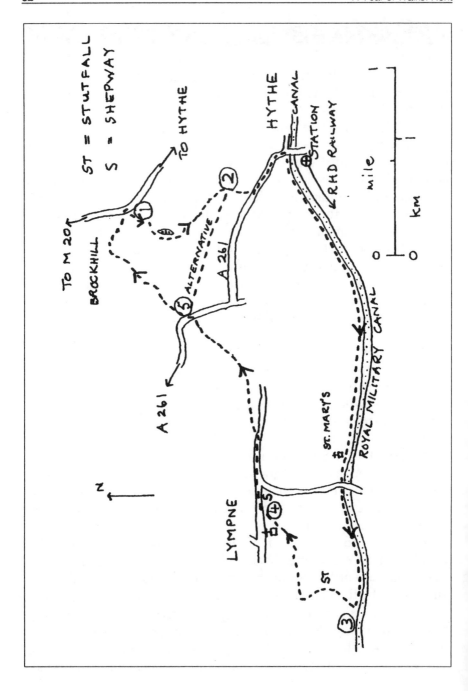

with the railway alongside us, on the opposite bank, for half a mile before it bends away towards Dymchurch.

To the right of our path is the steep slope of The Roughs, a grassland area which used to be the coastline. On the top of this will be seen an old quarry and a large communications dish in a small area used for military purposes, and then the imposing sight of Lympne castle. On this canal excursion, we pass a few houses and the large greenhouses of a Nursery, behind which are the remains of St Mary's church. Cross over the minor road at the foot of Lympne Hill – Shepway Cross is located up to the right – and walk through a small car park to continue straight ahead. There is a large rookery at the right side of the car park. A kingfisher or mute swans are amongst the birds which may be seen during the canal side walk.

Shortly after passing a dam on the canal, where a sluice gate opens out on a large drainage channel, look for the path turning to the right (3). Leave the canal side over a little footbridge, and climb up the hill. There are great views of the castle from here, as well as the ruins of Stutfall Castle, an old Roman fort. As we climb, the views over Romney open out, to reveal Dungeness power station and

Looking down to the Stutfall ruins on the former coastline at Lympne

probably the noise of trains and sight of the smoke rising from one of the steam engines which operate this line.

Stutfall castle was built to guard the port of Lemanis, at a time when the sea reached the foot of this slope. Some excavation of the site has taken place. It appears to have been affected by several earth movements, possibly small earthquakes, or merely soil slip. The ruins of the castle were used as an enclosure for horses, hence the name of stud fold, which became Studfall or Stutfall. Many of the stones from the ruins were used in Lympne Castle.

At the top of the steep climb, turn right along a horizontal path with trees on the left, and the steep slope and good views, to the right. The path we are now on is the Saxon Shore Way, and this leads into Lympne, to pass the castle, church and a car park (4).

From the church walk through the car park, along the surfaced driveway, passing a gate and follow the yellow arrow and the Saxon Shore Way sign. At the main road turn right, passing Shepway Cross erected in 1923, on the exact site where the Court of Shepway used to meet to discuss Cinque Ports business in the 14th century. About 400 metres along the road, just beyond the houses, go left over a stile and immediately turn right. After about 20 metres head diagonally left across the field, towards the corner of the wood – and following Saxon Shore Way. At the far edge of this field, do not follow the field boundary ditch, but head diagonally left on a grassy track across the field – with a communications tower visible on the North Downs scarp ahead. Just before the Oxenden Farm yard, go left across a small field, pass a duck pond and reach the A261 (5).

Turn left for 20 metres and then right at a post box on a stony track to the left of an old chapel (Pedlinge church) and on over the stile. Follow the SSW arrow, straight ahead across the middle of the field and through a kissing gate into the woods. This is Chesterfield Wood, private property but with a footpath leading through. Wild flowers thrive in this wood, and there is a rich assortment of trees too, mostly deciduous including a few damp-loving varieties. Notice evidence of former coppicing. Many birds may be seen and heard, with early chiffchaffs singing by the end of the month. Many summer visitors arrived quite early this year, brought in a spell of southerly winds.

Descend quite steeply and then level off through an area with primroses (and masses of bluebells later in the year). The clear path through the woods is still the SSW, as we reach a footbridge over a small stream and climb up the other side. The path bends to the right to become a broad grassy walk, with woods to the right and open fields to the left. Go through a gate and along a field margin, to reach an old kissing gate and emerge on to the road.

The SSW goes left, but we turn right, to pass Slaybrook, a magnificent old house, with a Historic Building of Kent plaque on its wall. Walk along the pavement, as far as Coach House and Old Stone Farm, and fork right through a narrow gap by a gate to enter Brockhill Country Park. The path immediately splits but fork right for the shorter route to the car park and the Visitor Centre, with its small snack bar.

Alternative walk – from Lympne.

Rather than starting in the Brockhill Country Park, this slightly shorter walk of 6 miles begins at Lympne, following much of the same route as the main walk, passing the railway station in Hythe and enjoying the leisurely and flat walk alongside the Royal Military Canal.

Follow the main walk above from point number 4 as far as Pedlinge chapel at point 5. The main walk leads on, to the left of this chapel, but we can go to the right of the chapel and along field margins, then passing to the left of a small wood, to reach a narrow path between hedges. The edge of Brockhill Park is to our left, and we soon descend to rejoin the main route at the stile mentioned as point number 2.

April

Dover

Kent can look particularly decorative in April, the month of nature's great awakening for the summer, when the blossom trees become very colourful, and a few can be seen even on this walk along the tops of the most famous cliffs in England. We look out over the busy English Channel with lively maritime activity, and on a clear day the coast of France can be seen. We follow good paths and tracks, for this undulating walk which contains two steep stretches, and two more if the extension walk is included.

Distances: about 7 miles for the first walk, and an extra 8-9 if the second or extension walk to Samphire Hoe is included, though there are several options available depending on energy and time available. There is so much of interest on this walk, that extra time can easily be spent on small sections of the walk.

Time required: 3-4 hours (or 7-8 for the full walk)

Maps: Landranger 179 Canterbury and East Kent, or Explorer 138

Starting Point: at N.T. car park (payment required by non-members of the N.T.) on Foxhill Down above Langdon Cliff GR336423. Leave Dover on the A258 towards Deal, and just beyond the castle look for the minor road turning right towards St Margaret's, signposted to the White Cliffs. About a mile along here turn right off the road, where the road is bending sharp left.

Amenities: Dover is the nearest town and is easily accessible by public transport. It has a wide range of hotels, pubs and cafes and a large Tourist Information Centre (tel. 01304 205108).

The Month

Weather

Noted for its changeability, the month lived up to its reputation in 1998, although with excessive rainfall thrown in too. This was the wettest April for 180 years (probably the wettest ever recorded in south-east England) – and rainfall was recorded in south-east England on every day of the month. Serious flooding occurred in several places. The longest known drought, from summer 1995 to winter 1997 is officially over, even though some water shortages may still occur. The problem is simply the fact that south-east England uses more water than its replacement rate. Daily maxima temperatures were mostly about 10°-14°C, but a very warm 16°-19°C from 20th to 23[rd]of the month. A few thunderstorms occurred, bringing to mind the old saying *"Thunder in spring, cold weather it will bring"* which may contain some sound wisdom, as it is the meeting of cold northerly air and mild southerly air which creates the conditions for thunderstorms. The Easter weekend, 10th-12th, was wintery, with lower temperatures and some ground frost. Snow fell to give up to 10cm on the North Downs, and Dover was made inaccessible for a few hours. There have been more white Easters than white Christmases in the last 50 years. The month ended with another cold spell of weather, brought on north and north-easterly winds.

The Countryside

Cold spells of weather, following on from the milder weeks which preceded, have serious effects on many plants and animals. For example hedgehogs come out of hibernation and then may be unable to find food when cold weather returns. Insects and butterflies which start moving, are suddenly affected by lower temperatures. However, whatever the weather, spring with its plants and birds appears as usual. The black buds on the ash trees are replaced by the purplish flowers which appear long before the leaves. Larch trees are showing their first tinges of very light green colour. Gorse and blackthorn line the paths in many places, and the small downland flowers which love the chalky soils are beginning to appear, including sheeps fescue, orchids, salad burnet. It is quite a yellow month on Kent motorways, with gorse as well as cowslips. Primroses are still in flower, as well as stitchwort and forget-me-nots, and by the end of the month many bluebells are seen. Some of the fields contain winter crops now growing up taller, but others are still brown from recent ploughing and spring crops will soon be planted.

Birds are becoming noisier and skylarks, pipits and finches are everywhere along the route, in the open fields and on the downland. The chasing season is in full swing in the bird world, not only in the hunt for food, but also with males chasing females, or chasing away other males. Sexy wing fluttering may also be seen, as many birds try to impress members of the opposite sex. A few of the song birds have started nesting and of course the magpies and sometimes crows will have started their onslaught on eggs and baby birds, though many of the small birds will lay again, possibly in more secluded nesting sites.

Along the Way

Fox Hill Down

Also known as Langdon Cliff, 21ha (52 acres) of chalk downland and scrub is owned by the National Trust. There are large parking areas, numerous footpaths and the Gateway to the White Cliffs Information Centre, with a snack bar. At the top of this hill is the Coastguard station, formerly a World War II battery with large coastal guns. Convicts were brought here in 1884, to work on the creation of the port, and a prison was built on the specially created terraces, now used for the car park. The site became an army barracks in 1908, and a battery of guns was located here in World War II, with guns which had a range of 8 miles.

Dover

The ancient town of Dover is a Cinque port, and has always had links with the sea. The famous white cliffs provide the first view of England, but also give excellent views across the water, to look out for enemies (or friends). The Romans called the harbour Dubris, and it was then in the estuary of the River Dour. By 1066 the original harbour had silted up and the ships moved further west beneath the cliffs. Henry VIII ordered the construction of a pier, but this encouraged the accumulation of shingle and a bar formed across the harbour. The Admiralty Pier of the 1840s prevented the accumulation of shingle and the present harbour dates from 1897-1909.

The castle stands on the site of an ancient earthworks and the oldest remains on the site now are the remains of the Roman pharos at 62ft (19m) high, but the top 19ft (5.8m) is medieval. The pharos, or lighthouse, is adjacent to the church of St Mary in the Castle which

Dover harbour and cliffs

dates from about AD1000, though in ruins in the 18th century and re-stored in the 1860s. Henry II's castle was begun in 1181, and beneath the castle is a tunnel system dug in 1216 at the time of an invasion from France. More tunnels were created during Napoleonic times and were used as air raid shelters and a military base during World War II. Hellfire Corner was the control room for the evacuation of Dunkirk.

On the other side of the town are the Western Heights, defences dating from Napoleonic times. Down in the town is the White Cliff Experience, which gives a pictorial account of the history of the town and recreates many of the major events. Almost next door to this building is the Painted House, built about AD200 just outside a great Roman naval fort, and only discovered in 1971. Much of it was buried under later buildings and this enabled the survival of a large area of Roman painted plaster, the best to be found anywhere north of the Alps.

South Foreland Lighthouse

Two lighthouses were built by Trinity House at South Foreland, the upper in 1793 and the lower in 1795, and both were rebuilt in the

Dover castle seen from the town centre

1840s. The lower was dismantled in 1904, but the upper is still a very distinctive landmark, and has been owned by the National Trust since 1989. It is open from April to October at weekends and Bank Holidays, 12.30-5.30pm and also open weekdays during school holidays. (01304 202756) Payment required.

The Lighthouse dates from 1843 and was used by Marconi for some of the first radio communications as an aid to navigation in 1898. A celebration on 24th December 1998 marked the anniversary of the very first ship-to-shore wireless communication. It is no longer in use as a lighthouse, but there is a model and exhibition inside.

The Pines Garden

It was Mr. Frederick E. Cleary CBE who founded the St Margaret's Bay Trust in 1970, whereby a group of local people aimed to improve the local environment. One of their obvious and major successes has been the creation of this garden in a very sheltered environment, on the site of an old rubbish dump. Officially opened as a public garden in 1971, it contains lawns, flowers, shrubs and trees, a lake and rock garden, and numerous seats which can be used by tired walkers. Outstanding features for me were the tulips round the trees, the myriad of tadpoles in the fish ponds, and the statue of Sir Winston Churchill. The garden also contains a small museum, and stone figures include busts of William I and of Julius Caesar, who landed at Walmer about 4 miles along the coast. The 9ft (2.7m) statue of Sir Winston Churchill sculpted by Oscar Nemon stands up on its plinth of Yugoslavian granite looking out at the white cliffs which he was so determined to defend against invaders.

Samphire Hoe

This new land at the foot of the famous Shakespeare Cliffs has been  created with rock obtained whilst digging out the Channel Tunnel. Engineers first came here in 1843 to create a platform along which the Folkestone-Dover railway runs. Also in the 19th century, early attempts were made at digging a channel tunnel and a little mining took place here too. Serious work on the tunnel began in 1987. The name hoe is derived from the Old English hoh meaning a ridge or spur of a hill, and samphire is a plant which was eaten as a vegetable, and still grows here but is now a protected plant. The car park is reached through a tunnel descending the cliffs, which were famous even in Shakespeare's time, and were referred to in King Lear:

Samphire

> There is a cliff, whose high and bending head
> Looks fearfully in the confined deep ...
> ... The crows and choughs that wing the midway air
> Show scarce so gross as beetles; half way down
> Hangs one that gathers samphire, dreadful trade.

Wild flowers and grasses were planted over half of Samphire Hoe and other plants will arrive on the wind to help encourage butter-

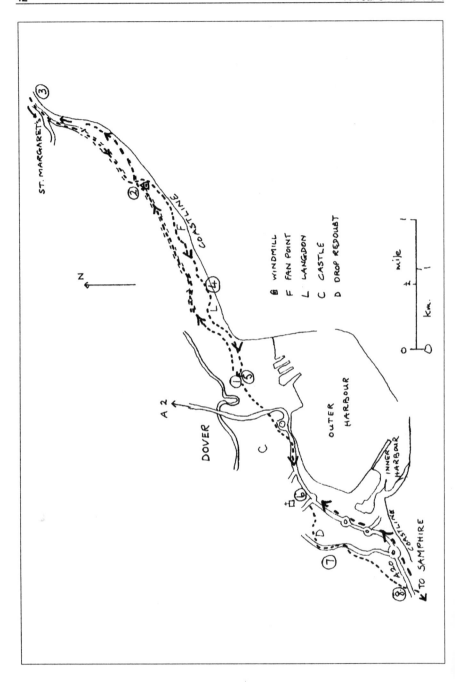

flies and birds. It is already a rich nature reserve, and footpaths stretch out along the length of the hoe, from the car park. Amongst major attractions in April are the yellow flowering cabbage, and the singing of the skylarks. Many other birds and plants can be seen on a walk around the hoe, and along the railway line at the foot of the cliffs, where patches of dense shrubby vegetation support linnets. On the hoe there are small wetland areas too, frequented by gulls and ducks.

The Main Walk

A large parking and picnic area (1) is available at the Gateway to the White Cliffs Information Centre. Walk eastwards from the end of the car parking area, on a path which immediately splits in two, with the right fork leading to a telescope and along the cliff top, and left fork going across a grassy area. Take this left fork as it climbs slightly, with good views of the Coastguard station, the masts and the radar scanner up to the left.

Rich and varied bird life will already be seen and heard, as we approach a kissing gate. Pass the N.T. sign for Langdon Hole, and bend slightly left, to stay near the fence marking the boundary of the scrubby grassland and the farmland. Another notice mentions that Exmoor ponies have been introduced to this area, to help control the scrub and maintain the chalk grasslands by their grazing. These ancient chalk grasslands are noted for their wild flowers, including cowslips, knapweed and salad burnet.

Langdon Hole with its grassy and scattered bushes is likely to have splashes of yellow, with gorse and wild cabbage flowers, and wayfaring trees will be coming into flower. Bird life may include a kestrel, and many summer visitors including cuckoo are likely to be seen or heard on this walk. We pass round the left margin of the grassland at the top edge of Langdon Hole, but gradually merge with the broad path coming up steadily from our right. This is the line of an old railway which linked the harbour area of Dover with Martin Mill, and was used for carrying building materials to the harbour, for the construction of the sea defences completed in 1909. It was partially restored for use during World War II, for rail mounted artillery.

Begin to climb slightly, and pass through a wooden kissing gate, with a Saxon Shore Way sign on it, and keep ahead on the broad track, now with fields on both sides. Notice the first of many bushes with the smooth wind-blown top sloping up from right to left, and often with the main trunk bending inland.

Reach a junction with a farm track, and turn right following the surfaced track through fields, losing sight of the sea for a while. Just keep going between fields, which you will notice are very stony, as we head towards the South Foreland Lighthouse. Skylarks will be singing lustily, whilst flying and coping with the wind which is likely to be blowing on this high exposed location, over 100 metres above sea level. Pipits too will be active in these fields. Germander speedwell and groundsel line many of the field margins.

Walk on to the left of the lighthouse (2), through the white gate to the crossing of tracks. Our return journey takes us to the right here, towards the cliff tops, but for the outward journey, keep straight ahead for 100 metres, to the next crossing of tracks. Turn right here along a stony track to pass Martlets, Dolphins Leap, the windmill and a few more houses, before reaching the N.T. sign for Lighthouse Down. Much of the down is still grass, but there are large areas of scrub, with colourful flowers and bushes.

Walk along Lighthouse Down, and begin to descend slightly, but note the dangerous exposed cliff edge – hang on to the children and dogs. At a point where the path is permanently closed turn left inland off Lighthouse Down and follow a stony track inland.

Turn right almost immediately, at the cross tracks, to descend towards St Margaret's Bay with houses on the right and The Pines Gardens on the left. Parts of the gardens can be seen from the road, but they are open daily and well worth a proper visit. Large white cliffs loom up straight ahead, beyond St Margaret's.

The track becomes a road and soon reaches the Bay Museum (tel. 01304 852764), on the right. Keep ahead to the main, though narrow road, and turn right to St Margaret's Bay, descending steeply past lovely houses and gardens. On the right, look out for a remnant of a flint wall dating from the times of the Napoleonic threat, 1798-1803. The Secretary of State, William Dundas, and the Prime Minister, William Pitt, ordered the construction of fortifications along this stretch of coast. The flinty shingle beach is crossed by groynes, which reduce the amount of longshore drift, and probably protects the cliffs from erosion. Cliffs of chalk tower over the beach. There is a beach cafe, and The Coastguard is a flint faced pub which can cater for all types of refreshment. However if you have a picnic, walk across the public car park to the benches overlooking the sea, or, if a cold wind is blowing from the north-east, sit on the beach behind one of the groynes. Think of the cross-channel swimmers, some of whom set out from this beach in the warmer weather of mid summer (3).

The return involves retracing steps past The Pines and after the road ends, keep straight ahead along South Foreland Valley towards the lighthouse. The lack of grazing has led to a denser growth of vegetation in South Foreland Valley, though this is excellent for small birds. Pass a cattle grid, and climb gently up, with more open ground to the right. At the second cattle grid note the hedgehog escape ladder. Our gradual ascent brings us out of the shelter of the valley, and we reach a narrow road and then the white gate by the lighthouse (2).

Just before reaching the white gate, turn left and pass the entrance to the lighthouse and keep going on the footpath leading towards the sea. At the cliffs, turn right and follow the cliff path to Dover, which is already visible in the distance. The route is roughly parallel to the outward route, but we stay close to the cliff top, accompanied by gulls floating lazily around and with the busy ferry traffic visible down in the sea below. Wild cabbage is in flower on the cliff edge, as well as wild wallflower, pink nettle and other flowers. Look out for sea birds, notably

Kittiwake

the gulls and kittiwakes which nest on the cliffs. A pair of peregrines has returned quite recently to these cliffs, and they find a ready supply of food. On your right will be land birds, and possibly house martins and swallows will be seen, especially near the end of the month, as they fly northwards along the coast, nearing the end of their long journey.

It is possible to walk straight on, down into Fan Hole and then up the other side, if you are feeling very energetic, but the main path bends inland round the deep hollow near Fan Point. The grassy slopes of the hollow are dotted with bushes, similar to Langdon Hole. Once beyond this natural amphitheatre, the path crosses a grassy area with small trees, several of which will be in blossom at this time of year. We then approach the exposed cliff top again, where we need to take care.

There is now a field on the right, and we reach a stile and a fence, beyond which is the area where the Exmoor ponies are being grazed. Either cross the stile here to skirt round the edge of Langdon Hole, or go to the left of the fence, to a lower stile at the bottom of the slope (4). On the cliff edge is the top of a steep zigzag path down 90 metres to the beach, dating from the time when gun emplacements were installed here. From the platform at the top of this path can be seen the protruding pieces of flint, often in clearly marked layers. They must be relics of a time million of years ago, when siliceous creatures died on the sea bed to form flint, whereas most of the dying sea creatures would consist of calcareous material which made up the chalk.

Go over this lower stile and continue across Langdon Hole, formerly an old water course, now a dry valley, as any water drains underground through the porous chalk. This hollow, like that at Fan Point, is similar to the valleuses overhanging the sea east of Newhaven, which form the famous Seven Sisters.

At the far side of Langdon Hole are several paths, but look for the lowest, the broad grassy route of the old railway, and walk along this, rather than climbing higher towards the path used on the outward journey. Follow this broad grassy path as it begins to descend towards Dover. Good views ahead to the town with the huge castle and church tower, and also clear views down left into the harbour are an interesting feature of this route. Go through a wooden kissing gate and notice remnants of old buildings on the left, and then small caves in the cliffs on the right, with rich flora showing a variety of colours especially in the spring.

As the path descends steadily, we reach an old concrete Public Footpath sign, and a white chalky path going up the cliff to the right (5). This leads up to a grassy area, above which is the car park where we began the walk. At the top of this narrow path is the time of decision, *either* to go on up to the right to return to the car park and the starting point near the Visitor Centre, *or* to take a longer walk.

From here an eight-mile walk will take us through the town, over the Western Heights, and then down to England's newest land on Samphire Hoe. This does involve some roadside walking in the town, accompanied by noisy traffic. Alternatively, it is obviously possible to park in the town to start the walk, and also is possible to drive through the tunnel down to Samphire Hoe for a short walk of a mile or two.

Extension, or alternative walk

This walk through Dover to Samphire Hoe could be started in the town where there are several parking areas, as well as frequent trains and buses. However, we are describing this as an extension from the main walk. For this extra walk, at the top of the narrow path bringing us from the old railway track, turn left towards Dover, to the path and then steps which lead down towards the road near the entrance to the Ferry Port. This path passes below the main A2 road (Jubilee Way) which bypasses the town centre, and follows the Saxon Shore Way signs to Atholl Terrace and then East Cliff, before reaching Townwall Street. To the left can be seen the harbour and then a sandy beach. Pass the Leisure Centre, the County Hotel and Tourist Information Centre (6), cross over the river and then turn right along Bench Street to the Market Square.

Follow the North Downs Way sign up to York Street, cross at the pedestrian crossing and turn left for a few metres, and then right up on to Adrian Street. This leads us uphill quite steeply, and as it bends round to the right, go left following the Saxon Shore Way and North Downs Way signs. Ascend some very steep steps towards the Western Heights, and reach the Information Board for Cowgate, which tells us that cows used to graze up here and the site of Betsy Trotswood's House was nearby. The steep 64 steps were built here to give access to paths and viewing points on the Heights for Sunday afternoon strollers.

Go through the kissing gate at the top of the steps and steeply on up a grassy slope. There is an information board for the Defensive Ditches just through a gate to the left, but we are really turning right here and ascending slightly for 40m to another information board about the Drop Redoubt.

There are excellent views into the old fortress, as well as across Dover to the castle. Inside the fortress was one of the pair of Roman lighthouses dating from AD43, and the second of these is still standing in the grounds of the castle alongside the church of St Mary in Castro. Together, they used to guide Roman ships into the harbour, which at that time was located where the Market Square is now situated.

Continue along the fence surrounding the Drop Redoubt, then turn left along the second side of the fortress. Where it bends again to the left, keep straight ahead across the level grassy area of the Western Heights Nature Reserve, with ribbons of Dover housing down to our right. Reach a kissing gate and an information board then descend the steps to the road where we turn left, following the NDW and SSW signs. Pass the left turn to the Grand Shaft, and the location of the former barracks. Grand Shaft barracks was the base for the soldiers manning the fort, and protecting the coastline, but access down to the harbour was slow, via winding narrow roads, so the Grand Shaft stairway was built, 1806-1809. Our route continues along the road, still following NDW signs.

Where the NDW is signposted to the right, follow this path which leads us over the edge of the hill and then down towards the main road, descending to rows of houses alongside the Old Folkestone Road (8). Reach this old main road via King Lear's Way, and turn right for a few metres, then go left beneath the A20 in a subway, and up the steps on the other side of this newish road. Turn right along the field margin nearly parallel to the road, and follow this path as it leads to the traffic lights at the top of the tunnel leading down to

Samphire Hoe. Walk down the path in the tunnel and stroll round a circuit of this new piece of land.

For the return, retrace steps as far as the subway beneath the A20, but stay on the right side of the road here, and continue as far as the first traffic island. From here, either side of the road can be followed, with the Western Docks, Hoverport and Marina on the right. At the third traffic island, on the left side of the road is the bottom of the Grand Shaft, which contains a stairway used by soldiers for a speedy route down to the foot of the cliffs. The return walk follows this main road towards the East Docks, and then along East Cliff and Atholl Terrace before ascending to the White Cliffs Visitor Centre again.

May

Westerham

The walk crosses the wooded hills and grassy vales of western Kent, and is almost a triangular walk between the three National Trust properties of Quebec House, Emmetts and Chartwell. This area is noted for trees, in spite of serious devastation during the so-called hurricane of October 1987; rhododendrons on the acid sandy soils; horses, and fine houses.

Distances: 9 miles, with short-cut option of 6 miles. Also, a 4-mile circuit along part of this route can be walked from the car park on Toys Hill GR470516.

Time required: 4-5 hours, though longer if visiting any National Trust properties, or only 3 if following the short cut.

Terrain: undulating across hills and vales, with a few quite steep hills. Several high stiles will be encountered, designed for long legged people.

Maps: Landranger 187 and 188 or Explorer 147.

Starting point: car park at the eastern end of Westerham, GR 449542. Westerham is on the A25 between Redhill and Sevenoaks, and is accessible by bus and by train.

Amenities: Westerham has a choice of pubs and cafes, and there are also facilities at National Trust properties on the route. Nearest TIC is at Sevenoaks (01732 450305).

The Month

Weather

Still officially a spring month, the lengthening hours of daylight in May normally help to ensure a few days of summery weather. However, the fruit growers of Kent, who are now fewer in number with the decline of orchards resulting from foreign competition, still have to be on the alert for a possibility of frost. The fruit blossom should traditionally be out on the 19th May, St Dunstan's Day. Legend has it that St Dunstan made a pact with the devil to spare apple and pear blossom on nine out of ten years, but on the 10th there will be a frost on St Dunstan's day. It can happen, though purely by coincidence, as frosts do occasionally occur in mid-May. In 1998, there were no real problems with cold nights, although the early part of the month was quite cool. There were warmer days in Kent during February than on some of these early days in the cricket season. However the land warmed up and as the angle of the sun rose, day maxima temperatures went over 20°C from the 8th-20th with long sunny spells. Temperatures were particularly high from 10th-14th, up to 28°C (with record temperatures for the month being recorded in several places), and a few thundery outbreaks occurred. Low-pressure systems dominated during the first week of the month, when day maxima were only about 10-15°C, but then high pressure built up over northern England and gave long hours of sunshine. The final week of the month became quite wet and thundery, and over one inch of rain fell in many places on the 28th, with the highest total being the 1.8 inches that fell in Margate.

The Countryside

Robert Herrick wrote:

> _First April, she with mellow showers,_
> _Opens the way for early flowers:_
> _Then after her comes smiling May,_
> _In a more rich and sweet array._

May is certainly richer in flowers and in growth of greenery, though in April the flowers may have seemed more exciting, be-

Horse chestnut

cause of their newness and appearance in a barer landscape. May is the time of sudden explosion, when everything is coming out, to the dismay of some hayfever sufferers. Crops are growing on the farms, trees are in blossom, and yellow rape is widespread, and sometimes rather smelly. Greenery dominates but there is abundant white in hedges and some of the trees, outstanding in many locations being the magnificent candles on the horse chestnut trees, which appear early in the month. These trees were first brought to Britain from the Balkans in the 16th century. A few of the horse chestnuts are of the variety with pink flowers. Life is also growing in the ponds where tadpoles are swimming around and moorhens are nesting. In many larger lakes, there will be ducks, coots, great crested grebes and the ever increasing numbers of Canada geese. Also, look out for the large nests of mute swans to be seen

Swift

in several Kentish locations, with the pen sitting on the eggs, and the male (cob) patrolling nearby keeping an eye on his wife, the nest, and possible intruders. Many of the hedgerow birds are disappearing from view in the greenery, though they are still singing so the males will be noticed. Overhead, swallows and house martins will be twittering as they search for insects, and the scythe-shaped wings

of the swifts will be seen by the middle of the month.

Along the Way

Westerham

On the Green are the statues of Churchill and Wolfe which dominate the centre of the town. In addition to Quebec House, Squerryes Court at the western end of the town has links with Wolfe, as he received his commission here in 1741, and there is a room containing Wolfe memorabilia. The bronze statue of Winston Churchill is by Oscar Nemon and the white marble plinth was given by Marshall Tito and the people of Yugoslavia in gratitude for Churchill's help in World War II. St Mary's parish church dates from the 12th century, with several alterations, notably in 1854 and a restoration in 1882. The tower is 13th century and is topped by a small shingle spire. The walls are of rubble and sandstone and the interior has some fine stained glass including a Burne-Jones memorial window to Wolfe. Fine windows and an interesting mosaic of the Last Supper are to be seen at the east end. The tower contains an unusual wooden staircase dating from the 14th century.

Quebec House

Situated at the eastern end of the town, this is now a National Trust property, where General Wolfe spent some of his early years. It is a fine 17th-century brick house, containing memorabilia of Wolfe and his family, and in the Tudor stable block is an exhibition about the Battle of Quebec, in 1759. The house is open from April to October, from 2-6pm on Tuesdays and Sundays.

Squerryes Court

At the opposite end of the town is Squerryes Court, a William and Mary manor house, lived in by the Warde family since John Warde bought Squerryes from the Earl of Jersey in 1731. There was an earlier house on the site in the 13th century, lived in by the de Squerie family, but this was replaced by the present building in the late 17th century. A wealth of paintings, porcelain and furniture can be seen in the house and the magnificent gardens are colourful throughout spring and summer. Many of the straight lines of the original garden, planned in 1709, can still be seen in the present paths and terraces. Open from April to September, on Wednesdays, Saturdays, Sundays and Bank Holidays.

Greensand Way

This long distance route with its oast house logo extends for 100 miles across Surrey and Kent, and the 55 miles in Kent link Limpsfield Chart to Hamstreet. The path was officially opened in April 1989. Much of the route follows the outcrop of the greensand rocks which were formed in shallow and brackish seas about 120 million years ago. The greensand is a type of sandstone which contains particles of the greenish mineral glauconite. The rock is generally more resistant to erosion than the neighbouring clays and so it often stands up and forms a ridge of high ground, much of which is covered by woodland. Toys Hill, at 245m, is the highest point on the Greensand Way in Kent, though Leith Hill in Surrey is the highest point along the Way.

Emmetts

This garden is located on the top of the hill, at a glorious resting point nearly half way round our walk. Situated at one of the highest points of Kent, the garden offers fine views looking out to the south, and since the devastation of the October 1987 storm, new views have been opened up. One famous tree which did survive the great storm is the 30 metres (100ft) high Wellingtonia near the house, the top of which reaches a height of over 250 metres above sea level, claimed to be the highest point reached by a tree in the whole of Kent. The fine collection of trees, shrubs and flowers is particularly colourful in spring, with daffodils and bluebells. Later in the year

Emmetts house with the tall Wellingtonia

are magnificent azaleas and a rose garden, and autumn colours are quite spectacular. Frederic Lubbock created the garden on former farmland, between 1890-1927. It covers about 2.5 hectares (6 acres) and has been in the care of the National Trust since 1964. Opening times are 11-5.30pm Wednesday-Sunday in April and May, and Saturdays, Sundays and Wednesdays, as well as Bank Holiday Mondays from June to October. It has a tea room and toilets.

Chartwell

This Victorian country house was the home of Sir Winston Churchill from 1924 until his death (1965), and the beautiful countryside in which it is set is thought to have provided him with inspiration as well as tranquillity. Churchill made many changes both to the house and the gardens. The rooms have been kept as they were in his time here, and contain much memorabilia. The study is where he did most of his writing, and in other rooms there are gifts he received from many heads of state, and also a selection of the uniforms he wore, including his famous siren suit. The gardens are magnificent, with lawns and flowers, and contain fish ponds as well as his studio. The Rose Garden was created by Lady Clementine. The house and gardens are open April to October on Wednesdays – Sundays and Bank Holidays. It is also open on Tuesdays in July and August. There is a restaurant. Easily accessible by car, but Chartwell, together with Emmetts and Quebec House is served by the Chartwell Explorer, a bus service from Sevenoaks, which runs at weekends and on Bank Holidays.

The Walk

To avoid going back on to the main road, take the footpath from the end of the car park (1) to walk into Westerham, signposted to Quebec House. Pass between houses, alongside the churchyard and then on to the Green, with the statues of Winston Churchill and Wolfe. From the statue of Winston cross over the main road and follow the Greensand Way footpath sign leading between shops, left of the Clothes Gallery along Water Lane, with a lovely garden on the left. Cross a small stream, over a stone slab and on to a worn stone step, then through a kissing gate and head up the hill, across the middle of the field. This is quite a climb up to another kissing gate, and then diagonally left across the next field, with Glebe House, on our left. Ignore the stile on the left, but just follow the left margin of this field. Keep going and drop down fairly steeply to the edge of the wood, and then turn left over the stile. Follow the edge of the wood as it bends round to the right, and where the path splits, fork left, still along the edge of the wood, and still following the circular walk and a Chartwell sign. Go left and follow the path through small deciduous trees on the right, almost parallel to the edge of the coniferous trees to our right.

At a split in the path, where there is a large gate on the right, we turn left, on FP380. We are staying close to the margin of the magnificent garden on the left, with its colourful rhododendrons and a wide variety of trees. This is Chart Edge garden and is open to the public on selected days, in May and July.

Pass the large house on the left, reach a road (B2026), and turn left along here for a few metres. At the entrance to Chart Edge cross the road (2), towards the old school, and then turn right on to Hosey Common. Follow the footpath sign into the woods, passing trees planted by the Duke and Duchess of Kent on 23rdMarch 1988, as replacement for those lost in October 1987. Follow the main path through the woods (FP 381), a fairly straight path heading southwards through Hosey Common and then bending left to go east. There is a confusion of paths, but aim to keep straight on, following marker posts with a yellow arrow. Cross a slight dip and then climb up past a post, in an easterly direction. The narrow path leads through silver birch trees, with a few tall Scots pine to right and left. Reach a cross-paths and keep straight ahead, still following the yellow arrow, to emerge on a narrow road (still on FP381). Footpaths throughout Kent are generally well signed, and in many locations their official numbers can be seen on the marker posts.

At the minor road, leave the common, pass Brackenwood on our right and walk into the attractive hamlet of French Street. At the T-junction by a couple of houses, turn right, passing an old burial ground, with a yew tree, and after a further 50 metres reach the two paths on the left (FP307 and FP309), opposite a post box (3). Go over the stile, heading eastwards and take the right fork of the two, going steeply downhill. This is along FP309, also on the Weardale Walk, a circular walk which goes round from Chartwell to Emmetts and back. At this stile, 307 is signposted to the left, and 309 to the right.

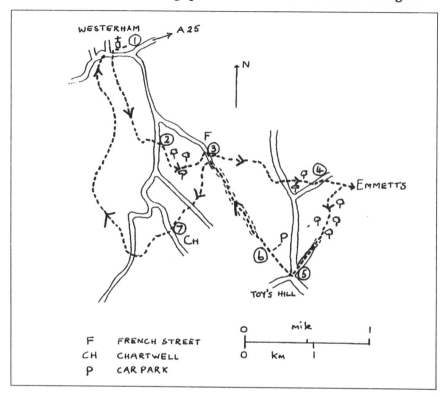

Short cut

For the short-cut route, which reduces the walk by about three miles, do not go over the stile but carry on along the road for a further 50m, passing Apple Tree Cottage on the right. Just beyond this house, turn right, on a signposted bridleway. The longer route rejoins at this point, by coming along the road from the opposite direction (but turns left).

Walk along the drive to Mannings Wood, and when this forks left towards the house, keep straight ahead along the grassy track between hedges. At the end of the hedge on the left, turn left, on the Weardale Walk and the Greensand Way. This may be a muddy path, between hedges and then trees, but soon widens slightly. After a quarter mile in the woods, reach a narrow road, where the Weardale Walk turns left, we keep straight ahead on the left of the two choices. This is still the Greensand Way and enters more woods and begins to descend quite steeply. Pass a large house with stables on the right, and as the path levels off slightly, notice the lakes and gardens of Chartwell to the left.

Descend to the road, where the entrance to Chartwell is just to the left (7), and this is well worth a visit if you have time. Our walk keeps straight ahead, across the road, and climbs the steps to head steeply up into more woods, where many fallen trees are still in evidence, relics of 1987 and other recent storms. Many of the fallen trees, which may appear dead at first sight, have surprising amounts of new growth coming out from fallen main trunks. Follow the marker posts for the Greensand Way (and FP365) still climbing, and as the path levels off near the top of the hill, pass a right turn (FP399) and then a left turn (FP368), to reach a fence where we turn right. The path soon divides and we take the right fork to descend steeply to a road (B2026). On the left is the N.T. sign for Mariners Hill, a small property partly given by Octavia Hill, one of the founders of the N.T., who lived in Crockham Hill nearby.

Cross the road and walk along the driveway to April Cottage. The track to the cottage goes left, but we fork right, and then the Greensand Way goes left up hill, but we keep right again, in a north-westerly direction, on the level path into the woods. Bluebells and other flowers such as red campion are prolific in these woods. When the path splits, keep left, that is nearly straight ahead, and descend slightly along a sunken track, to reach the boundary fence of the garden of the house on the right, Crockham House.

Reach the end of the wood and go over the stile and straight on across the field, noting a secluded house tucked away up to the left, along the margin of the woods. Go over a stile at the end of the field and on through the next field, with the woods just a few metres to the left, and the small River Darent at the bottom of the field to the right. At the end of this field go over the stile by an iron gate, and after about 50 metres turn right along the track, between fields. As this track bends left, go left over a stile into the field we have been walking alongside, and then turn right to walk down the valley, passing several small lakes on our right. These are fishing lakes on the Squerryes Estate. Walk through the buttercup meadows, with warblers and other birds singing all around, to reach a stile by a gate. Carry on along the track, to another stile and gate, where a footpath joins us from the left (the Greensand Way link). Continue along the stony track, passing Park Lodge on the left, and then the millpond with a pair of swans, to walk back into Westerham. Just before reaching the main road, take the path leading to the right, if you wish to avoid walking alongside the busy main road. Either way will lead back to the Green in the centre of Westerham.

Main walk

Heading east along the Weardale Walk, we go down steeply to a foot bridge, with large barns and oast houses to the right, at French Street Farm. Go up the hill and over a stile and across the track, following the Weardale Walk signs to reach the road, Chart Lane.

Go straight across this road and continue along a track winding through the woods. These mainly deciduous woods are very colourful in spring, with carpets of wild flowers. Reach a road, Emmetts Lane, and ignoring the path going straight across, turn left for about 90 metres and then right (4) to follow the footpath sign heading due east on to N.T. land. This is The Chart, and the clear path passes between silver birch trees and dense undergrowth. Reach a major cross-tracks, with blue arrows pointing right and left, and our onward route is to the right. But first, go straight on for about 50 metres to reach a stile and then between rhododendron bushes to emerge into Emmetts, with its magnificent gardens and wonderful views over the lowlands to Bough Beech Reservoir. This lake was formed in 1969, along a small tributary of the Eden, and is popular for fishing, sailing and Nature Conservation.

Retrace steps from near the Stable Tearooms, and 50 metres past the first stile, turn left along the cross tracks referred to earlier. Follow this stony track between oak and silver birch, and go down hill to a major cross tracks. Ignore the left turn going steeply down but keep straight ahead, following Weardale Walk, and begin to climb, in a sunken track. Reach a cross-paths and continue ahead following the blue arrow and still climbing. Much of this area was badly damaged in the Great Storm of 1987, but has been left untouched to see how it recovers. Go on over the top and begin to descend, slowly at first, through quite a lot of holly trees. Reach a cross-paths, where the Weardale Walk turns right to join the Greensand Way, but we keep straight ahead and descend steeply.

Go on down hill straight to the road and turn right to follow this to Toys Hill settlement at the crossroads (5). For the onward walk we are turning right just before the telephone box, but before doing so, walk for about 100m along this narrow road, Puddledock Lane, to visit the memorial well to Octavia Hill. She sank this well for the use of the villagers in 1898, and it contains the quote from Psalm 104 verse 10, *'he sendeth the springs into the rivers which run among the hills.'* The well was restored in 1999 by the National Trust with assistance from the Octavia Hill Society and the Beckenham and Bromley Centre. Sit at the well for a moment and enjoy the views across the Weald to the South Downs.

Then retrace steps to the telephone box and begin to climb immediately, on to the slopes of Toys Hill. By the N.T. notice board for Toys Hill the path splits – take either way as they merge again fairly soon, just before a major cross-paths. At this cross-paths (6), the orange route comes in from the right, from the Toys Hill car park. But we just keep ahead along the Greensand Way bridleway, following it north-west, out of the woods, into the valley with woods on the right. The stony track (Greensand Way) leads past French Street Farm and French Street Oast. The oasts here are square topped, rather than the usual conical shape, and date from the early 19th century.

Climb steeply as the track becomes surfaced, and the winding road passes the garden of Holly Tree House on the right, with its wonderful display of rhododendrons – and there is honeysuckle on the wall of the house. Pass a sharp turn to our left, near the top of this climb – the drive to French Street House. The next left turn is where we join the short-cut route, leading us up past Mannings Wood on to the grassy track, and along the route already described in the short-cut alternative above.

Short alternative walk, from Toys Hill

At 245m (800ft) this is one of the highest points in Kent, and many trees, including some more than 400 years old, were badly damaged in the storm of October 1987. There is a large car park (GR470516) on the narrow road from Brasted to Toys Hill, and a good starting point for a walk. For a four mile circuit passing French Street, Emmetts and Toys Hill village, set off from the far left corner of the car park (as seen when coming in from the road). Pass the Information Board and follow the orange arrow and the Greensand Way sign. The path is also signed to Octavia Hill's Well. Walk through the trees to reach an open patch with a seat, commanding wonderful views out to the south and south-west. Go steeply on down hill, to reach a cross-paths (6) where we can join on to the main route described earlier. Turn right at this cross-paths and follow the Greensand Way bridleway to French Street. Do not turn left up to Mannings Wood, but keep straight ahead along the narrow road to the post box and point number 3 on the main walk. Follow the main route to points 4, 5 and 6 to return to Toys Hill and complete this circuit.

June

Chilham to Canterbury

Through the orchards of Kent, and a few hop fields too, we follow part of the route of the Pilgrims on their way to Canterbury. This walk takes us through a landscape showing the best of English scenery, with rich farmland, patches of woodland, hectares of orchards, hops and field crops. The tiny villages with some thatched houses and converted oast houses, are used by city workers now and not by farm labourers.

Distances: Chilham to Canterbury 9 miles, or Canterbury to Chilham 7 miles, or for a long walk on a nice summer's day, join them together for the full 16 miles.

Time required: 7 hours (or 3-4 if travelling one way by train, rather than on foot), plus time for Chilham, and even more time to be spent in Canterbury

Terrain: an easy walk with no steep hills but merely a few gentle undulations. There are a few stiles though some also have adjacent gates.

Maps: OS Landranger 179 or Explorers 137 and 150 with a small section on 149

Starting point: can be at either end, but our description is from a start at Chilham, where there is a large car park (GR 067536). If you plan to use the train for part of this walk, there is a small car park at Chilham station, and a larger car park at Canterbury West station. There is a local bus service as well as the regular train service from Canterbury to Ashford.

Amenities: Canterbury is the nearest town, and has a large Tourist Information Centre (01227 766567). Refreshments are available in Chilham, Chartham Hatch, Chartham, and Canterbury has a large choice.

The Month

Weather

Although often referred to as flaming June, this month can be cool and wet if the weather is predominantly coming from the west, or cool and dry if northerly weather prevails. Even though the sun is at its highest in the sky and the hours of daylight are longest, June has not often been a hot month in recent years. In 1998, temperatures in

Kent were reaching a daily maximum of up to 20°C. early in the month, but a cool spell in mid-month saw maxima at only about 15°C., and the 11th June was colder than last Christmas Day in several locations. Thankfully, temperatures did rise to over 20°C. from the 17th June onwards. The month was very wet with over 4" rainfall, though this was not as wet as in the previous year. Very wet days occurred in the first and last weeks and the 14th received well over an inch in many places. The tennis championships at Wimbledon were affected by rain though not as seriously delayed as in 1997. However, the good news was that there were no hosepipe bans this year. An old weather saying which might have some relevance is:

A dry May and dripping June
Brings everything in tune.

Certainly, by the end of the month, the countryside was looking lush and prolific and sunshine in July could ensure a good harvest after an excellent growing month.

The Countryside

Small apples are appearing on the trees, and the cereals are growing up to waist height, but not yet turning golden. Many fields are crossed by the straight lines of tracks created, where the tractors have barged through the crops to spread the several doses of fertiliser or pesti/insecti-cides. In a large field there is a considerable area of unproductive ground along these wheel tracks! The roadside

Honeysuckle

verges and hedgerows are prolific with wild flowers, including daisies, jack by the hedge, herb robert, wild strawberry which you may be able to identify. Each week sees a change in this profusion of wild flowers, but throughout the month the nettles will be growing well, with the threat of problems to come when walking in July. Honeysuckle is climbing through many of the hedges, and wild roses are coming into flower. The whitish field rose is scentless and has longer trails than the dog rose which is pinkish and usually sweet scented. The name 'dog' originated because it is regarded as a common or valueless flower. Another flower equally abundant in many places is the elder, a hedgerow shrub which rapidly grows into a tree.

Walking in late June, at the time of the summer solstice and the longest day of the year, assures long hours of daylight, a wonderful bonus for walkers. The longest day is the 21st or 22nd of June but the name of Midsummer Day is often given to the 24th. It is frequently a misnomer, as summer has generally only just begun by this date. However the birds are very active, whatever the weather, with skylarks, warblers, yellow hammers, linnets, chaffinches and thrushes all singing, as well as spending time collecting food to feed to hungry chicks. Swallows and house martins will be rushing about madly, and keeping up their non-stop twittering.

Along the Way

Canterbury

An excellent starting and/or finishing point to a walk, with all its attractions and places of interest. There is the cathedral of course, but also a Heritage Centre; the Canterbury Tales, a Medieval adventure depicting Chaucer's band of Pilgrims and the tales they told; the ruined castle; the remains of St Augustine's Abbey; the old West Gate; Greyfriars; many other buildings; and walking tours with a guide can lead you round the town centre if you wish.

Chilham

The centre of village looks like a film set, and has often been used as such. It has won the Best Kept Village in Kent Award – and there is very strong competition for this honour. The village square is surrounded by ancient buildings, mostly from the 17th and 18th century. In the 18th century several buildings were refaced in brick, and have been half timbered since then. Tea rooms and the gift shop are popular calling points, and the White Horse pub is 15th century. A narrow

In the square at Chilham

road leads out from each corner of the square, and there is a large car park on the road which leads to the A252. Adjacent to the square is the castle, a 17th-century Jacobean mansion, with the octagonal keep of the 12th-century castle nearby. Magnificent gardens surround the castle though these are no longer open to the public except on a few special occasions.

St Mary church

This 14th-century church is of flint and sandstone ashlar, with notable 19th-century stained glass windows. Amongst the numerous interesting features inside the church is the early 17th-century memorial to Sir Dudley Digges, in Bethersden marble, a local stone which can be cut and polished. Notice the 19th-century sculpture of the Hardy children, showing children's toys. The stump in the churchyard is all that remains of the yew tree which had survived for 1300 years, but was fatally damaged by falling trees in the great storm of October 15, 1987. The stump is kept as a memorial to John Edward Harding, Church Warden from 1976-87. The early Georgian vicarage is in the north-east corner of the churchyard.

Chartham

The cruciform 13th-century St Mary's church has a roof of oak, and contains some good stained glass windows. Many of these were renewed in 1801, but some date from about 1294. An impressive brass of Sir Robert de Septvans dates from about 1306. Also in the village is a large paper mill - a mill has been on this site since the 14th century, using water from the River Stour which flows in two channels here.

Bigbury Camp

This camp is described as a major earthwork, a univallate contour fort, covering 13 hectares (33 acres), and probably dates from the early Iron Age. It is possible that it was overrun by the forces of Julius Caesar on his second visit to Britain in 54BC, when he was trying to move inland after landing at Walmer. Once he had progressed, he established the foundations of Canterbury on the Stour marshes. Late Iron Age domestic objects have been found on this site, as well as iron slave chains and chariot equipment. Much of the hill is covered by coppiced woodland, managed in a traditional way to encourage a variety of wild life.

Harbledown

Described as ' bob up and down' in 'The Manciple Tale' by Chaucer, the village is now a suburb of Canterbury. The famous spring and the church with adjacent almshouses are passed on the walk. Harbledown has two churches, St Michael and St Nicholas, and St Nicholas has a sloping floor, supposedly so that the floor could be washed down after the service for lepers.

Stour Valley Walk

This walk follows the river from Lenham to Sandwich, via Ashford and Canterbury, passing marshes and reedbeds, as well as woods and downs, and fields of fruit and hops in places. The symbol is the heron, likely to be seen somewhere along the route, and there is a heronry in Chilham. England's largest colony of herons is at the RSPB Reserve at High Halstow in Kent.

The Walk

The full walk is from Chilham to Canterbury and back, but either half can be walked separately, using the frequent train service to return to your starting point. If just taking the half day walk from Chilham to Canterbury, start by taking the train from Canterbury West station to Chilham travelling along the valley of the Great Stour, with its old gravel workings, now lakes much appreciated by birds, and by bird watchers. From the station in Chilham, walk to the main road and turn left towards Godmersham and Wye for 100 metres, then cross over and turn right to walk up into the village. Pass the Woolpack Inn, the old forge which has been used as a book-shop, and reach the square in the centre of the village, alongside the entrance to the castle. Everything is neat and tidy, and very picturesque. If starting from the car park in Chilham, just walk up into the square (1).

From the corner of the square near the White Horse Pub, the walk follows the North Downs Way through the churchyard. Pass the old yew stump which is thought to date from about 690 AD, and walk along the left side of the church to an information board about Chilham and the North Downs Way. Leave the churchyard by the small gate and walk down Church Hill, the narrow road from the corner of the square to the busy A252. Cross straight over (quickly), and walk along the minor road, then over the crossroads and straight on along the narrow winding road leading to the delightfully named Old Wives Lees. You may have noticed the shell symbol on the Pilgrim Way road sign, and the acorn symbol of the North Downs Way. Although walking along a road, this is a very rural scene, with orchards alongside the road, birds singing noisily, and abundant wild flowers on the verges. The main road is soon forgotten and the main noise will be the birds. The sun will probably be shining too!

At Old Wives Lees turn right, along Lower Lees Road (also called Pilgrims Way), following the signpost to Chartham and Canterbury, passing the Post Office on the right. When past the houses on the left and the old converted North Court Oast House, soon fork left along an narrow road and after 30 metres (2) go on to a narrow path leading between lines of trees. Walk between orchards and then past old hop fields, and at a track turn right for 30m and then left, to climb up

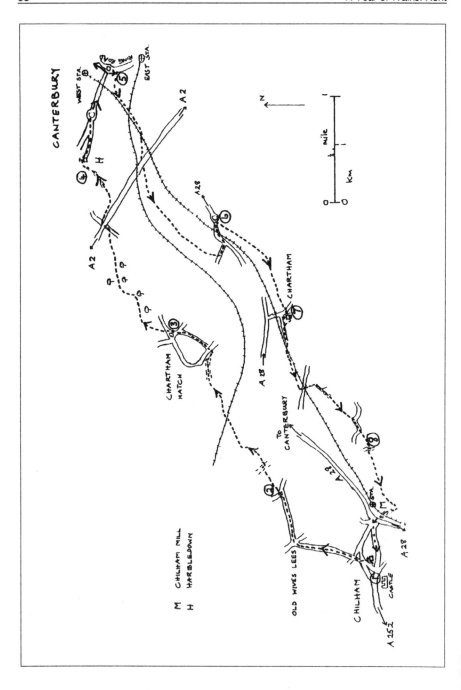

alongside a line of beech trees, crunching the beech mast underfoot. The Stour Valley lakes are visible to the right, as you follow the edge of this field round to a stile, and this leads to a path through orchards. There may be piles of boxes around here, just waiting to be filled with fruit at harvest time.

Cross over the railway line (from Canterbury East to Faversham and Sittingbourne) and follow the track and then a narrow surfaced road, leading to the right of Nickle Farm and the two oast towers of the old barn, and cross the track and continue on up the hill. At the concrete track turn left, and pass two houses with immaculate gardens (and one small swimming pool), then fork right where the track splits and walk past the radio mast and building with three oast towers to reach a road. Turn left for a few metres and then right, along New Town Street, to pass the Chapter Arms, with good food and a Dovecot (unrelated facts). Roses are colourful all round the gardens and the doves are murmuring quietly to themselves. Walk into Chartham Hatch, looking to see if many of the houses still have house martin nests under their guttering.

At the end of New Town Street, turn left (3) and then take a narrow path between gardens through to a road. Go straight across, to the edge of a playing field, and fork right through a kissing gate, following the NDW sign. The path leads by the backs of gardens and into the woods and soon reaches an orchard to the right of the path. At the end of this orchard, fork left through more woodland, including a large number of sweet chestnut, and signs of coppicing. There are many wild flowers here especially in the spring, and recently cleared areas will probably be passed, as the woodland is ever changing. This is inevitable in all managed woodlands, and in the recently cleared areas there is often dense undergrowth, and many small trees notably silver birch which are often early colonisers. This is a superb environment for small birds. Reach a major track. Here there is a N.W.D. Information Board about Bigbury Camp on the hill up to the right.

At the road turn left and walk over the noisy A2, and then immediately turn right along a concrete track parallel to this main road. This soon narrows to a path and passes between an orchard and the A2. Go up a small hill and as it levels off, go left over a stile through a

The Black Prince's well

Coat of Arms seen on the arch of
the well

windbreak, and cross over the high point of the field. Head towards the right corner of some trees, and reach a concrete track. Follow this downhill between windbreaks and orchards, with views ahead to the two churches in Harbledown, and an oast house. As we level off, cross a small stream to soon reach a stile and gate, then pass the modernised oast house.

Follow the track, and at an old gate turn sharp right (4), towards St Nicholas' Hospital. Walk along the tarmac drive, passing the Black Prince's Well on the left. Note the feathers of the Royal Arms on the top of the arch. It is claimed that the Black Prince drank at this well on his last journey from Canterbury to London.

Keep going up this small hill and come to the churchyard and almshouses. The almshouses were the Ancient Hospital of St Nicholas Harbledown, founded by Archbishop Lanfranc about 1084, for the relief of lepers. When leprosy disappeared from England, the hospital gradually changed its use to almshouses.

Walk on through the gate to the road, where we turn right, to pass the Old Coach and Horses on the left, and then the flint St Michael's and All Angels Harbledown church, part of which dates from AD1050. Reach the main road where we turn right, as the impressive sight of the cathedral comes into view. Follow the main road, past the first island and along the straight road, Rheims Way. Reach the Ring Road at the island and, if intending to return to Chilham by train, turn left here for Canterbury West station (note there is also a Canterbury East station, which does not have trains to Chilham).

The walk should end at the cathedral, a fitting finale for any walk, as it was for the Pilgrims in years gone by. There is the memorial to Thomas à Becket who was murdered here in 1170, as well as the tombs of the Black Prince and King Henry IV. Modern tourists are attracted here in greater numbers than the pilgrims of the past, and many foreign languages are likely to be heard. The city has been a commercial centre since Roman times, and Saxons came here after the Romans left in the 5th century. In AD597, St Augustine established the first Canterbury cathedral as well as St Augustine's Abbey.

For the walk back to Chilham, retrace steps to the island on the Ring Road and turn right, still following Rheims Way. After about 200 metres turn right at a wooden gate (5), cross the grassy area to a wooden arched bridge. Head over to the right, following a footpath sign, through the children's play area as far as the toilets. Then turn left along a tarmac lane between hedges, following the Stour Valley Walk sign. Alongside this lane is dense undergrowth and small trees, ideal for wild flowers and birds and butterflies. Hops and blackberries will be growing over the hedges later in the year.

Pass beneath a railway bridge, still on a surfaced lane, and soon cross the railway line at a level crossing. When the narrow road bends right beneath a high tunnel, which carries the railway line from Canterbury East, we turn left following the Stour Valley Walk sign and the Centenary Walk 1889-1989, and go over a small ditch and beneath the A2. The path bends right and we walk on between orchards, pears on the left and apples on the right. Notice that most of the trees in the orchards are quite small, for ease of picking, unlike the taller trees which were common 20 or 30 years ago.

A path goes off to the right through the orchard and we pass Tonford Manor on the left, but keep straight ahead through a gate and along the track. Reach a narrow road where the Centenary Walk turns right, but we keep straight ahead through more orchards for half a mile, passing a lake on the left before reaching Howfield Farm. Pass to the left of the farm buildings to the road where a sign tells us that the Newma Fruit Company is here, and we turn left. A small industrial estate is on our right, and Howfield Manor on the left, as we walk out to the main road, A28. Turn left along the road for a few hundred metres, passing over the railway bridge and just before the river bridge, go right, over the stile, to follow the riverside path (6). This is still the Stour Valley Walk, and we follow the riverbank for just over a mile to reach Chartham. The river is on our left, birds and dragonflies are likely to be seen, and there are several lakes, former gravel workings, on our right, which are very rich in bird life.

Reach a playing field on our right, and then the road, where we turn right. On the left at this point is the Chartham Paper Mill and further along beyond the mill is the village pub, The Artichoke, serving good food if required. There has been a mill here for centuries, but the present large building is dated 1949. To the right are the church, village shop and the station, but we only go as far as St Mary's church (7). Pass through the churchyard and out to a narrow road and a small village green beyond. We follow the narrow road, but notice over to the far side of the green some very interesting houses, notably Bedford House dating from AD1420 and formerly the home of Douglas T. Snarr. It merits a Historic House of Kent plaque.

Walk on over the river bridge and along the straight road, nearly as far as houses and a large mill, and as the road begins to bend left, we turn right at the footpath sign to cross the railway line via two kissing gates. Turn left and walk along the field margin, parallel with the railway, with hop gardens to the right. Further over to the right, on the hillside, is the route of our outward walk, where we were 3-4 hours ago.

At the end of the field go over a stile and on to a drive where we turn left, to reach a road. Turn left and pass over the railway and then turn right on a narrow path which leads through to a large field, with more hops. Turn left along the field margin, as far as the narrow road where we turn right. When this road bends left, we keep straight ahead along a track and then across the middle of a large field, possibly with flax, very blue in early summer, or dingy brown in later months. In mid-field the path splits, with the Stour Valley Walk going up to the left, but we keep straight ahead here, to a gate and a narrow road.

After a straight stretch along the road, where it bends right we go left over a stile and straight ahead across the field to a marker post on the left side of the strip of trees. This leads us to a stile and across the right margin of a garden to another stile, and on to a narrow farm road (8). Turn right here for a few metres, then left just before the farm buildings, through a gate and alongside the right margin of the field. When the hedge ends, go right for 30 metres and then left along the tree-lined field margins, with another lake in a former gravel pit beyond the trees. To our left is a large field – probably with cereals, sloping up to the woods.

At the end of the field, go through the hedge and turn right on a narrow path going downhill through the trees, to descend to the river, with the old but modernised mill across on the other side. There has been a mill here since at least the times of Domesday, and this present mill was constructed between 1830-1850, and is five storeys high. It was taken over by the Mid Kent Water Company in 1960 and has been beautifully restored. Pass the house on the left and then turn right on the driveway to the mill and just continue to the level crossing. Go beyond this to the road, and straight across up to Chilham Village.

July

Lamberhurst and Scotney

A modern castle and a moated ruined castle, as well as two churches and some typical Wealden scenery are to be seen on this walk.

Distances: 10½ miles, with two shorter options of about 5 miles each.

Time required: 5 hours, or 2-3 for the shorter options. Do find time to visit the ruined Scotney castle.

Terrain: paths and tracks, (with the possibility of a few muddy patches) and quite undulating with some short climbs but no long hills.

Maps: Landranger 188 or Explorer 136.

Starting point: from the car park at Scotney Castle, just off the A21 one mile south of Lamberhurst GR 686354. The car park in Lamberhurst can also be used as a starting point GR676362. Bus service from Royal Tunbridge Wells.

Amenities: The nearest town is Tunbridge Wells, which has several pubs and restaurants, and a Tourist Information Centre (01892 515675).

The Month

Weather

An average sequence of weather would give low pressure systems passing over northern England and Scotland, whilst the south of England receives a ridge of high pressure and drier weather. 1998 was not quite true to the average, but a very wet month over the north was not matched in the south-east, where rainfall totals were quite low. Wet and windy spells brought over half an inch of rainfall on the two wettest days, the 12th and 21st, but otherwise much of the month was a mixture of cloud and sun.

If the first of July be rainy weather,
'Twill rain, more or less, for four weeks together.

The first of July was a dry day, and so too was St Swithin's Day, the 15th, and the month was generally dry though dull and cloudy, unlike the previous four Julys which were quite sunny. Daily maxima were mostly from 18-23°C and the only really hot day was on the 20th when 27°C was reached because of a strong burst of southerly winds. Although there was a pleasant warm ending to the month, there was a strong feeling of a very poor summer, especially as April and June had been so wet.

The Countryside

The landscape has remained much greener than in an average July, though some of the cereal crops are beginning to ripen and wild grasses are showing first signs of browning. Occasional fields of rape and flax give a yellow or blue colour to break up the green appearance of the fields. There is plenty of variety of colour on field margins and hedgerows, but the profusion of nature in the hedges and on the roadsides gradually changes during the month as some of nature begins to wind down after the hectic growth of May and June. But wild flowers are still abundant, and wild geranium and nettle-leaved bell flowers are amongst the most attractive, with thistles adding a purple colour, and meadowsweet giving the white.

Ragwort

Ragwort is beginning to add bright yellow to waste ground and chalklands. This last plant, though very colourful, is seen increasingly as a menace and a campaign has been launched this year to control this plant by the use of sprays, using experience gained in USA and Australia. This invader from Egypt thrives in poor soils and is a rapid spreader, each plant producing as many as 150,000 seeds, which can lie dormant for years before germinating. The plant is highly toxic to horses, cattle and sheep, causing liver damage, and many horses have been affected by hay containing ragwort. Although most of the nesting season for birds is over by the end of the month, there are many fully-grown young still hanging around to be fed, and in the case of wood pigeons and collared doves, the nesting season is still in full swing. House martins too are still feeding chicks in the nest, though many fledgelings are sitting around hoping to be fed for a few more days before having to fend for themselves. Bird song has diminished, but yellow hammers, robins and wrens are still giving the occasional burst, but it must be for pleasure and relaxation, as the birds are not trying to attract mates at this time of year or even setting up territorial claims for the winter.

Along the Way

Scotney

The castle was probably named after Walter de Scoteni, and was built in 1378 by Roger de Ashburnham as a fortified Manor House. The moat was created by damming the river, and forming two islands. It is a 'fairy tale castle on an island in a lake' and was the home of the Darrell family for 350 years. There is a fragment of the 14th-century moated castle, as well as the new house built for Edward Hussey III in 1837-44. Hussey had advice on siting the house from Rev. William Gilpin (who believed that Capability Brown's landscapes were too smooth and tidy), and Anthony Salvin was the

Ice house at Scotney

architect. A sandstone quarry just below this house provided much of the building stone. The castle stands in the valley of the River Bewl and magnificent gardens make use of the steep slopes of the valley sides, which are accentuated by the excavation of the quarry. There is a thatched ice house near the castle, and this used ice taken from the moat in winter. Winters must have been colder in those days! Christopher Hussey the grandson of Edward Hussey III, died in 1970 and left the house and the estate to the National Trust. The estate covers 315 hectares (770 acres), and visitors are able to walk on a network of footpaths on the estate. The castle garden is open from the end of March till the end of October, daily except for Mondays and Tuesdays (though open on Bank Holiday Mondays). The old castle is open from May to early September.

Lamberhurst

The village may have grown because of iron ore, and certainly a part of the famous Wealden iron industry was located in this area, using power from the River Teise and its tributaries. Lamberhurst has been more famous for vines in recent years, though one large vineyard has closed. In addition to its 14th-century church, it contains many old buildings. The impressive village street is still complete, and as it was in the past, with tile walled houses, weatherboarded houses and half timbered houses all to be seen. One of the oldest buildings is the Chequers Inn, dating from 1412. Coggers Hall is an old Tudor building which housed weavers many years ago. St Mary's, a sandstone church is 14th century but is on the site of a much older building. The tower and timber roof in the nave date from the 15th century, but much of the present building was restored in the 19th century. There is a boot scraper outside the church, which hopefully you will not require.

Vineyard

Kilndown

The Christ Church in Kilndown is neo-Gothic, designed in 1841 by Anthony Salvin who also designed the modern Scotney Castle. Alexander Beresford-Hope, from Bedgebury, soon changed the original plain design to an example of the Gothic revival. Pulpit, screen and altar are amongst the many interesting features in this church, as well as several colourful windows, even though a few of the windows were shattered by bombs in World War II. Pews and stalls were carved by craftsmen from the Bedgebury estate who also created the marquetry panels at the rear of the church. The churchyard contains several ornate tombs of the Beresford-Hope family.

The Main Walk

From the car park (1) walk back to the drive, pass a pond on the right and some rhododendrons, and the speed restriction of 20 mph. After 100 metres go right, up a few steps into the woods, following the Woodland Walk. This mixed woodland is rich in bird life and the path leads us through to a stile. Go straight on here across a field, signposted towards Lamberhurst, and head towards the corner of a woodland area. Bear slightly left alongside the fence and climb gently up to the top of the hill. Turn left through a wooden pinch stile and then right along the field margin for 30-40 metres to a traditional stile where there are good views across to Lamberhurst church, Court Lodge and the golf course.

Once over the stile (2) turn left alongside the hedge and descend quite steeply to the bottom of the field, then proceed through a gateway, across a grassy patch to the edge of the golf course. Turn right along the edge of the course for about 100 metres then turn left across the fairway to walk along the right side of a line of trees. This leads us to a stile in a hedge and beyond here we cross a fairway, watching out for golf balls coming from the left, to reach a gap in the fence and walk on across a playing field. The buildings of Lamberhurst can be seen ahead. On the left of the field is a small playground area, and we pass the cricket pitch before reaching a gate, small car park with toilets and recycling bins, before arriving at the main road (3).

Turn left for about 20 metres then take the right fork, towards Wadhurst and Bayham Abbey. Climb steadily, and once past the houses and just before the road splits, look for steps on the right, and a footpath leading up into an orchard. Apples and vines have been growing here although on my most recent visit the vines were not productive. The straight path leads through the orchards and joins a farm track coming in from the left, but we just keep straight on, admiring the long views ahead and to the right. Pass the buildings of Ridge Farm on our left, then an oast house up to the left, and arrive at a hedge, like a T-junction. Turn right for a few metres and then left, down some steps to a concrete track, where we turn right. Follow this track downhill, and cross over the small River Teise.

A few metres beyond the river is a cross-paths, and just before the straight ahead path begins to climb, turn left on the flat, passing an old building and walk along the field margin, with the hedge on our right. At the end of the field cross the river again, over a metal footbridge with a low single bar at each end, and cross the field to a gate and out on to a track. This is the site of the old furnace, and we pass between buildings now used as stables and a modernised oast house. Go on through a gate, pass an old barn and continue along the track, cross over the Teise again and on along a surfaced driveway to walk through to a narrow road (4).

Turn right past the first house which is the magnificent Oast House, and then at the second house, turn right along the drive at the concrete footpath sign, and follow the hedge on the right, through to an open patch and then a stile. Go over this and across the middle of the field to a gap in the hedge and then diagonally left across the next field (probably cereals), noticing the oast house up to the left. There are several old converted oasts in this area, as well as a few fields of hops, part of the traditional scenery in this picturesque and picture book part of the county. Reach the corner of a wood, and turn right alongside it, with trees to the left and the large open field to the right. Reach a stile in the corner of the field and keep straight on, to a gap through a line of trees at the end of the next field. Woods are about 30-40m up to the left, and over to the right are views of the countryside we crossed half an hour ago, on the outward walk.

Head up to the top left corner of the field, cross a green track and

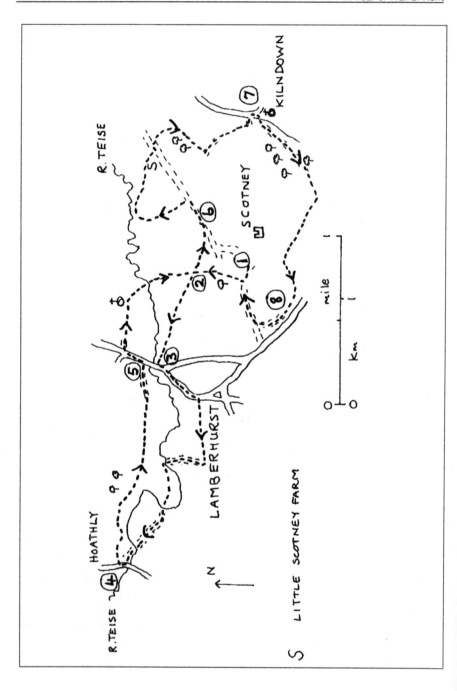

keep straight ahead along the left margin of the field to reach the stile in the corner, in a hedge. Walk on along the left margin of the next field, through a gap at the end of that field, and after a few more metres, bend right across the field towards the bottom right corner, just to the right of a large barn. Here we join a track on the valley floor and turn left to follow this track between hedges to soon reach an industrial factory yard. Keep straight on between houses to reach the A21 in Lamberhurst (5). Our onward route is to the left, but the Chequers, and George and Dragon are to the right, if required.

Turn left up the hill, passing the Old Forge, now making fireplaces, and the village school with its clock tower, and the narrow road leading to Owl House Garden. The War Memorial is on the right and shortly beyond this is the wrought iron sign for Lamberhurst, with its grapes, sheep, horse and oast. Cross over and turn right here, along a driveway leading to Court Lodge. The surfaced footpath soon veers to the right off this drive, and leads us past this three-storey 18th-century sandstone house and into the churchyard. St Mary the Virgin has a commanding site on the hillside, with all round views.

Walking away from the church door the onward route is to the bottom left corner of the churchyard, where there are two footpaths. Ignore the left turn, which goes across the field close to the two huge Wellingtonia trees which have survived man and weather, but take the other path downhill to the River Teise, again. Once over the sturdy footbridge, the path splits and we take the right fork to climb steadily. The golf course is away to our right. Cross the drive to Pierce Barn, with the house a few metres to our left, and follow the hedge on our left as we approach the top of the hill, where we have been before, early in this walk (2).

Go over the stile and back into Scotney Castle Estate, and straight ahead for about 40m then left through the wooden pinch stile. At the finger post where Scotney is pointed to the right, go straight ahead towards Kilndown, and stay close to the left margin of the field. Reach a gate and continue along the next field, following the hedge as it leads down to a gate and stile and the surfaced driveway. Our starting point in the car park is only half a mile to the right – if a short cut is required.

However, the onward walk is around the Estate, so we turn left, and soon pass a stile and path to Kilndown going right across a grassy field to the stream. We continue along the drive to the end of the field on the left (6), where a gap in the hedge enables us to turn left on a sunken track between fields. At the top of a slight rise are good views left to Lamberhurst, and ahead can be seen the traffic on the A262, with a small isolated church just beyond. Overhead there is likely to be traffic to Gatwick airport. Descend slightly along the left margin of the field, to a stile, and then on downwards towards the river, with the trees of Foxbury Wood on the left. Turn right along the flat valley floor, with the River Teise on our left, and hop fields across on the other side.

At the end of the field, go through the gate and alongside the hedge with another field of hops to our left. Reach a gate and head diagonally left across the field, to a stile, and then alongside the left of the next field, with Little Scotney Farm and the oasts up to the right, to another stile and the driveway. Go left for a few metres, over the bridge and then right over the stile. Head straight across the middle of the field and then steeply up to a stile and into Broadham Woods.

Little Scotney Farm

The clear path leads through the woods, and emerging from the edge of the wood, we leave the signed path to turn right along the edge of the field, with the wood on our right. At the end of the field and the wood, turn left along a drive, which has been gullied by rainwater. Many tree roots are exposed along the sunken driveway. We climb steadily along this drive, and just before it bends left, go right following a green arrow, through a few trees to a stile and diagonally across a small field to another stile and a path into the Kilndown Woods. After about 50m into the woods reach a slightly sunken track where we turn left. Follow this track between numerous coppiced trees, and gradually bend round to the right, and reach a main track where we turn left. After a few more metres pass through a gate and out on to the road in Kilndown, opposite a house which was formerly a pub (7).

Turn right here, but after about 20 metres go right along a track between a house on the right and the Quarry Centre on the left, following the signs to Scotney Estate. Before setting off along this track, it is worth going a few metres along the road to visit the remarkable Christ Church.

From the church, retrace steps to the telephone box and the Kilndown Quarry Centre, and turn along the track signposted to Scotney Estate. Pass a pond on the left where there was a small quarry which supplied some of the rock used in building the church. Enter the woods, soon passing a few houses on the right, with their access road on the left. Keep straight ahead, to reach a fine line of beech trees in a more open space, then pass another isolated house and begin to descend slightly. These beautiful woods are rich in flowers and birds, and seem remote from the world, even though there may be a little traffic noise ahead and to the left. Ignore tracks going off to the right as we progress along this woodland path following signs to Scotney Castle.

At a major cross tracks, turn right along what is the Old Carriage Drive, originally the main driveway to the castle. The track splits but we keep straight ahead through a white gate, and out into more open parkland. Descend slightly to a level patch, and over to the left, beyond a fence and a few trees is the old wagon pool, where carts were driven to cool their wheels, especially in hot weather. Pass another white gate, copies of the original gates designed by Anthony Salvin and over the stone bridge to cross the River Bewl, where there are good views across to the modern castle. Just before the next bridge turn left along the field margin, and on our right is the small Sweet Bourne which feeds the moat around the ruined castle. At the end of this field, and just before reaching the main road, A21, go right over the stile and down the steps to cross the bourne on the stepping stones (8), at the site of the old ford. Climb up the steps on the other side, and follow the path and then the track in between the buildings of workshops and timber yard. Pass another white gate and continue along this drive nearly as far as the main road, then turn right along another track which soon splits but keep straight ahead. Climb up through the trees and at the top of the climb reach the driveway, which is the main entrance into Scotney. Turn right here and follow this driveway back to the car park and the starting point.

Short walk from Scotney

For a five mile walk around the estate, leave the car park (1) and pass the walled garden on the left, then the toilets and the National Trust Regional Offices. Follow the driveway as it winds away from the buildings, to pass between fields. On the left is a wood in which there is a pond, and shortly beyond this, a path comes in from the left. This is the route of the main walk which can now be followed (6 – onwards).

Short walk from Lamberhurst

The full walk can be started in Lamberhurst but for a shorter circuit of about 5 miles, start at point 3 on the main walk and follow this route for just over three miles to point 5. Then, either turn right and walk through the village back to your starting point, or continue for another two miles along the main walk past the church and up to the next hill to point number 2. Here, instead of going over the stile into the Scotney estate, turn right and follow the instructions in the early part of the main walk, from point number 2 to point 3, crossing the golf course to the car park in Lamberhurst.

August

Wye

The flat valley floor of the Stour Valley, the narrow steep valley of Devil's Kneading Trough and the plateau surface of the North Downs provide three differing landscapes on these walks across delightful Kent countryside.

Distances: 6 miles from Wye, or 5 miles from Broad Downs. The two walks can be combined for a total distance of just over 8 miles

Time required: 2 to 4 hours

Terrain: extends from a flat valley and up and down a steep scarp and across undulating North Downs in a river valley on the dip slope.

Maps: either the OS Landranger 189, or the Explorer 137.

Starting point: the free car park in the centre of Wye GR 053468, or on Broad Downs GR 079455. Bus and trains services from Canterbury and Ashford.

Amenities: Nearest town and Tourist Information Centre (01233 629165) is Ashford. Choice of refreshments in Wye.

The Month

Weather

A very lush and green landscape is usual in August, as this is often one of the wettest months of the year, but in the occasional very dry years (e.g. 1989,1990) the landscape may have a more brown and parched appearance. 1998 was a very dry month in south-eastern England though much of the weather was westerly. After storms on the first of the month and an unsettled first week, there were several sunny days, when daily maxima rose to 27°C or 28°C from the 6th to the 11th of the month (with 32° recorded at Gravesend). Otherwise, daily maxima throughout the month were only about 20-21°. Sunshine totals were slightly below average, about 500 hours instead of the average of about 590.

There are several old weather sayings relating to the 24th August, St Bartholomew's Day, including *'this is the day to start bringing in the honey.'* St Bartholomew's is one of the Days of Prediction, when weather patterns might be forecast. In most years this is said to be a time of settled though cold and dewy weather, when gardeners should think about bringing in their delicate plants. This may turn out to be true some years but is not a reliable forecast, and neither is the old saying that *'very hot weather in the first week of August presages a hard winter.'*

The Countryside

This is the month when most walkers are out on the paths, and yet it does not require more than a few minutes walking to get away from crowds and into the quiet countryside which is still looking colourful at this time of year. Although the most popular walking month, because it coincides with school holidays, there are often seasonal problems to be encountered, and overcome. Tall crops of wheat or barley, or even broad beans, may be leaning across the paths, until harvesting has taken place. Many paths are overgrown with nettles now reaching head height, and the brambles are spreading menacingly. However this is still a good time to get out in the countryside. The centre of Wye is ablaze with colour, and on the nearby downs can be seen a variety of wild flowers including the delicate harebell, blowing in the wind. Clematis vitalba or traveller's joy is hanging in profusion, forerunner of the old man's beard

Traveller's Joy

Cuckoo

so common in downland in the autumn. The white flowers of greater bind-weed are also common, if you wish to squeeze them and play 'granny pop out of bed'. Yellowhammers may be seen or heard along the hedgerows of the Stour Plain, but many birds are beginning to moult and remain half hidden and at low profile, very different from their behaviour in the early summer, when hunting for territory and for a mate. A few summer visitors are still around, but the earliest to go, the cuckoo and the swift will depart by the middle of the month. But-terflies are abundant, in sunny weather, especially around buddleia bushes, and dragonflies too are numerous.

Along the Way

Wye

A delightful place to start or finish a walk, this small market town is a very old settlement, dating from pre-Roman times. It is dominated by the 13th-century St Gregory and St Martin church, which once had a tall spire that was struck by lightning in 1572. The central tower fell in 1686, and damaged much of the church. The present tower dates from 1701. Archbishop John Kempe, a Wye man, and Archbishop of York and Canterbury, was involved in redesigning part of the church. Adjacent to the church is Wye College, founded by Kempe in 1447, originally for training priests. It is now part of London University and a nationally important Agricultural College. Wye College owns 400 hectares of land around here, and farms about 300ha, the remainder being gardens and woods, providing ex-

The church of St Gregory & St Martin in Wye

perience in the environmental management and conservation courses. Paths are well kept and signed in the Wye College fields, and hedges are well cared for, as part of good farming practice. Look out for the various types of windbreaks on their estate – conifers, poplars or hawthorn.

A second local of distinction was Mrs. Aphra Behn, born here in 1640, who was a spy in Antwerp for Charles II. She later became a professional writer, very unusual for a woman in those days, and she is buried in Westminster Abbey.

Devil's Kneading Trough

Several deep hollows called coombes can be seen on the scarp slope of the North Downs and similarly on the scarp face of the South Downs (in Sussex). One of the deepest and steepest is the Devil's Kneading Trough, shaped about 10,000 years ago, by water and ice activity rather than the efforts of the Devil. This magnificent valley results from the freeze thaw activity and water erosion during the Ice Age, at the time this area was experiencing a tundra climate similar to parts of northern Canada or Alaska today. Water in the rock froze overnight and then melted during the day. The expansion and contraction this caused gradually cracked the rock, and small fragments broke off from the top of the rocks, thereby exposing fresh rock for the process to act upon. The broken fragments slipped off down to the bottom of the slope, where accumulations occurred. As the hollow became bigger the freezing and thawing could attack more rock. The process is most rapid where the rock already has a line of weakness such as a joint or a fault.

National Nature Reserve

The reserve contains over 100 hectares of North Down escarpment, managed by English Nature. Wild thyme, common milkwort, knapweed and oxeye daisy and several orchids are amongst the flowers to be seen, and you may catch a glimpse of one of the snakes or lizards which live here, but they are very timid and generally manage to remain hidden. Butterflies are numerous, common blue, meadow brown and others, and the black and red six-spot burnet, a day flying moth, is common. Kestrels hunt around here, and many small birds such as skylarks and meadow pipits are feeding out in the open grasslands. Warblers still inhabit the woods nearby, but as they are not singing at this time of year, are not easily seen in all the greenery. Several varieties of tits may be heard, as well as nuthatches, green woodpeckers and jays. Opened-up hazelnuts may be seen on the ground, where squirrels have been busy.

Around the Trough are areas of small trees and scrub. Left to itself the scrubby vegetation would take over from the grassland and many of the grassland flowers and insects would totally disappear. Management is vital, and both cutting by hand, or by using sheep, enables the grassland plants to survive. Even rabbits may be welcome as they perform the same service as the sheep in grazing and preventing larger plants from growing.

The Crown

On the grassy slope of the North Downs scarp is a memorial crown which can be seen from miles away. It was carved in the chalk by students at Wye College in 1902, to commemorate the coronation of Edward VII. It became overgrown but was restored in the early 90s by a grant from the National Westminster and the MAFF.

The walk from Wye

If starting from the car park begin by walking in the wrong direction towards the Victorian railway station (1), to admire the 17th-century stone bridge over the River Stour and perhaps visit the Tickled Trout on the river bank. The bridge is on the site of a ford, used on the ancient North Downs track, and near the same point was a water mill, recorded in the Domesday Book.

From the bridge, walk along the main street past a shop on the left and the school on the right and the Wye Village Hall. Beyond Church Street and the Wife of Bath Restaurant, where the road bends left, go right along Cherry Garden Lane. This narrow road leads past a few houses and out of town, passing the Wye Cricket Ground and the playing fields of Wye Agricultural College. All the land around here is part of Wye College, and Withersdane Hall on the left, is a students' Hall of Residence, built in the 1950s. Views of the North Downs have opened up to the left, with the Crown quite prominent.

The path runs along a road for 50 metres and then keeps straight ahead on a track through fields. When the track narrows to a path we still keep straight ahead along the edge of fields, passing Silks Farm just to our right, and over to the left at the foot of the scarp are the farm complexes of Coldharbour and Amage. After following the series of field boundaries, we then cross the middle of a field, and as the soil becomes lighter and contain more flints, we climb slightly, approaching the foot of the chalk escarpment. The soils on the Downs are very different from the clayey soils of the plain.

At the end of this field (2) go over the stile on to a road and turn right. On the left is a stile to a Wye College Estate Walk, with an English Nature National Nature Reserve Information Board. Keep going to pass Pickersdane Cottage on the right, with its typical Wealden architecture of hung tiles and boarding and a lovely garden with a stream, fed by a spring. Fork left at the junction, on the road to Brabourne, and climb steadily. At the top of the hill, go left up the broad path, which might be muddy to start with, but soon becomes drier and flinty. Overhanging trees encourage a rich bird life, and flowers are growing on the banks. Climb up steadily to a gate at the top, where we turn left and join the North Downs Way, to walk along a grassy field. Follow the fence, with a steep slope down to the left, to reach a stile beyond which is the Devil's Kneading Trough – a deep coombe, almost gorge-like in its steepness. This coombe has a grassy floor but with rougher grasses and some bushes on the slopes, where small terracettes expose the underlying chalk. Erosion and land slip is a serious danger here, which is why the steep slopes have been fenced off. The grassy downland on our right is the popular picnic and playground area of Broad Downs, with two car parks, to get visiting cars off the narrow road. Kite flying and lazing in the sun are popular activities here, and it was here that Dr. Coggan, Archbishop of Canterbury officially opened the North Downs Way, in 1978. There is a restaurant, the Devil's Kneading Trough, located just across the road to the right.

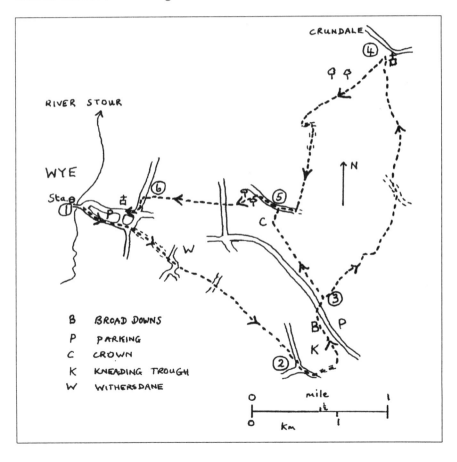

Walk on past the Trough, ignoring a gate to the left, but passing through the iron kissing gate following the NDW arrow. The clear path heads through a small wooded area, the top edge of Pickersdane Scrubs woodland, with ash, hazel, oak, hawthorn, beech and sycamore amongst many other trees. Occasional glades encourage the growth of flowers and grasses, thereby supporting many butterflies too. We soon reach a stile and cross over the road, to a surfaced track (3), and after a few metres at a gate on the left, is the onward route back to Wye.

Go through the gate and after about 30m pass through a second, and larger gate, following the North Downs Way acorn, to walk along the top edge of a long grassy field. You pass, and ignore, two foot-paths going to the right. The field has its daisies and poppies, flutter-ing butterflies and singing birds, and glorious views open out to the left, across the farmed fields of the Stour valley floor. The fields are showing all the possibilities with stubble, fields already ploughed (possibly with gulls following the tractor), grassy fields with cattle, a hopfield, greenhouses and woodlands in a patterned and well cared for landscape. Climb over a stile (with a small doggy gap to the right) and on to the hummocky surface of an old quarry, where slightly down the slope is the Wye Crown, with a fairly new flint lining. At the end of the grassy area, by a log seat, turn right over a stile, sign-posted the Shepherd Neame walk as well as NDW. Walk along the edge of a field (with a wood on the left) to descend a few steps to a stile and a minor road (5), where the Broad Downs walk comes along from the right.

Turn left along the road, going downhill, where the banks are lined with wild flowers, and after about 300m, where a narrow steep valley can be seen to the right, fork left, along a fenced path. Walk into the The Junipers woodland, where many trees suffered badly in storms of 1987, including some of the trees which had been planted to commemorate victory in the Napoleonic wars. Descend the scarp slope, with abundant flowers and birds to be seen or heard in the woods. Emerge into an open field with Wye clearly visible half a mile away, and Ashford over to the left. Straight across the Stour Plain is the slope of the North Downs, curving round and away to the west. Walk alongside the hedge, cross the road and notice the Stour

Valley Walk going off to the right, but keep straight on, to pass green-houses and the Meteorological Station of the Wye College (6).

At the main road, turn left on Olantigh Road, admiring the magnolia grandiflora on the college wall. Turn right at the crossroad, passing the main entrance of Wye College and then the church on the right, with the ice cream shop and a supermarket on the left, to arrive back at the starting point.

Starting from Broad Downs

The car park is at the road side, near the Kneading Trough Restaurant. Walk back along the narrow road to the point where the North Downs Way crosses the road (3). Turn right here and pass the gate on the left, which is the route of the Wye walk, and just keep straight ahead. Follow the narrow lane, a surfaced track heading north-east, and downhill between large fields, generally of cereals, to Coombe Manor. About 50m before reaching the buildings, turn right along a footpath following the margin of a field, and at the end of this field, go left through an old iron gate to walk alongside the fence for 70-80 metres. Continue through a large iron gate on to a narrow path between hedges, with some trees and masses of wild flowers. Expansive views open up to the left, and Hurst Wood slopes up to the right.

Reach the end of a large field and keep straight ahead, passing to the side of the large gate, and continue near the edge of the woods, with another huge field to the left. Look out for some twayblade growing on the left of the path. This greenish member of the orchid family has a pair of green leaves, and is often associated with old established woodlands.

Reach a track (linking Pett Street Farm with the nearby road) and turn left for a few metres then right, into trees again, but soon to emerge in the open. Walk along the right margin of the field, with trees to the right and farm buildings and houses down to the left. Go on through a large iron gate, and keep straight ahead, now on the left margin of the field, with grassland stretching up to woodland on our right. At a stile, go over and then along a path in the woods, and when we emerge from the trees continue along a grassy track. Keep straight ahead, until the track bends left down to the bottom of the valley, just before reaching the end of the field, where we join the valley floor track. Go through a gap in the hedge to continue along the left margin of the next field, by a line of trees, with the open fields sloping up to the right. These are remnants of Crundale downland, considered to be amongst the best, most isolated and most glorious of all the Kent Downs.

Reach a large iron gate (4), beyond which is a meeting of paths, including a right turn to visit St Mary's church Crundale, a flint church standing all alone and apparently quite isolated. But our route ahead is along the narrow path, going left, just before the large gate, and descending steeply a few metres through shrubs, into a field. The path leads across the middle of the field, to a stile and hedge, then across a surfaced track and across the middle of the next field towards the corner of the woods. From the corner of Marriage Wood (the name marriage is derived from the words moere hyreg = boundary ridge) carry on uphill steadily, with the wood on the right and open views to the left.

Join a track and pass through a small wood, and straight ahead through the next field, still climbing slightly. As the path levels off, pass a small pond on the right, and reach the far corner of the field. Once out of the field, just before the open space where paths meet, turn sharp left along a track between hedges. Follow this to the buildings, and beehives, then turn right, through a large wooden gate to pass the entrance to Marriage Farm. Walk along the stony farm drive, between fences at first and then alongside open fields on the right and trees on the left, to reach the isolated house, Lone Barn, and the narrow road. Turn right along the road, and after about 200 metres reach a point where a stile and a few steps are on the left (5). The route to Wye is straight ahead, but to return to Broad Downs go left here, walking above the memorial carved into the hillside, and following the North Downs Way back to the starting point.

Longer walk

If wishing to combine the two walks described, for a walk of just over 8 miles, begin in Wye and follow the route as far as point 3. Then follow the Broad Downs walk as far as point 5 before picking up the Wye walk again, to complete the circuit.

September

Hollingbourne and Leeds

Farmland, woodland, the downs and parkland are all part of these walks, and there may be special entertainment created by one of Kent's major tourist attractions, Leeds Castle.

Distances: Hollingbourne to Leeds 6½ miles; Hollingbourne to the North Downs Way 5 miles; to combine the two walks would be a distance of 9½ miles.

Time required: 4-5 hours for the combined walk or 2-3 hours for the shorter options.

Terrain: Gentle walking with undulations over small hills but a steeper climb up on to the North Downs.

Maps: Landranger 188 or Explorer 148

Starting point: Hollingbourne, grid ref 844551, where there is parking. This is reached to the left off the M20 (about 4 miles beyond Maidstone) at junction 8, follow the A20 towards Lenham for nearly a mile and at an island, where The Jarvis Hotel is on the right, turn left to Hollingbourne, through Eyhorne Street. Railway station at Hollingbourne; bus service from Maidstone

Amenities: various pubs on the route – e.g. The Park Gate on the A20 (formerly used as stores and domestic quarters for the staff from Leeds Castle), The Dirty Habit in Hollingbourne, also pubs in Eyhorne Street. Nearest town is Maidstone, where there is a Tourist Information Centre (01622 602169)

The Month

Weather

The North Sea is generally at its warmest in September, and this can affect the weather in Kent if winds come from the east. This year the sea has been slightly warmer than average and probably helped to produce more moisture in the county, notably the fog and low cloud during the third week. The early part of the month saw some rain almost every day, and daily maxima temperatures were generally in the low 20°s. They then became lower for a few days, before creeping above 20°C again from the 19th onwards. A sunny spell was experienced from 20th-25th, as high pressure ruled the weather.

An old weather lore saying for this month, which must have occurred one year in the past, but is generally not reliable is:

Fair weather first day of September,
Fair weather for the month.

September is unlikely to be settled and anticyclonic throughout the month, though there is generally at least one spell of sunny weather, as seen this year. The month is also likely to bring more varied and unsettled weather, though less so than the western parts of southern England, unless isolated and sudden storms occur. One famous example was at Guildford in Surrey, not far away from Kent, which received 50mm in 24 hours on the 10th September in 1976.

The Countryside

This is still a green month, and even at the end of September, only a few trees were showing signs of autumnal colouring. Grassy fields on the North Downs are a lighter shade of green than the pasture fields on the lowlands, where grazing is important because of the large number of horses in this area. There are a few large prairie-like fields, where cereals have been grown for a few years, both on the clay soils of the flatter lands at the foot of the scarp, and also to the north of the scarp, on the dip slope. Stubble remains in a few of these fields, which is very useful for the flocks of larks and finches. A few of these cereal-producing fields have already been ploughed, and tractors can be seen followed by gulls. Large flocks of gulls were seen in many places, often enjoying feasts of craneflies, which have been very numerous after a wet summer. What has happened to the rooks which used to be the prime followers of farm tractors? Around the margins of the fields the hedgerows are changing colour, with yellows beginning to appear in the midst of the greens, and red berries of hawthorn and hips. These are not evidence of a cold winter ahead, but a sign of a good summer, and in this year's case, a wet summer. There is also the distinctive sight of Old man's beard or traveller's joy (clematis vitalba), especially to be seen on the chalky areas. The feathery seed heads are appearing and *"the downy seeds of traveller's joy fill the air ... and appear like insects on the wing"* (wrote Gilbert White in 1788). Bird life at this time will still include a few summer visitors, especially warblers flittering about in the shrubs and hedges, and swallows and house martins overhead, hunting for the insects which are so abundant at this time of the year. Many birds are flocking, the swallows and martins prior to migration, but the starlings and finches ready for winter. The field margins and lanes have many lovely wild flowers still on show, though growth has slowed, and they are mostly fading by the end of the month. The farmland around Hollingbourne has a lot of pasture, for horses as well as some sheep and cattle, but quite a few arable fields too.

Gulls, rather than rooks, follow the tractors nowadays

Along the Way

Hollingbourne

All Saints church is of ragstone and flint, some blocks of ashlar including a few of sandstone. It has a fine tower and was much restored in 1876 by G.G. Scott. The church contains memorials to the Culpeper family who lived in Hollingbourne Manor during the 17th century. The Manor is a 16th-century brick house, planned as an 'E' shape but the north wing was never built. The King's Head has an 18th-century front, with chequered brick, and the Malthouse has some half timbering with overhang.

Leeds Castle

A wooden castle was built here by the Saxons in the 9th century, and later the Normans built one of stone. The ownership of the castle changed hands several times, and it was altered and enlarged over

Main gate to Leeds Castle

the centuries. The present castle has been described by some as the loveliest castle in the world, and it is certainly one of the greatest tourist attractions in Britain. It was named after Led, who was a Minister of Ethelbert IV, and stands on two islands in the middle of a lake formed by the River Len, a tributary of the Medway. Many Kings and Queens have lived here, including Edward I (who gave the castle to his wife Eleanor of Castile) and Edward III, and it was King Henry VIII who spent vast sums on turning the existing castle into a luxurious palace. It was bought in 1926 by Hon Olive, Lady Baillie who restored many of the rooms to the former medieval style. The Parkland around the castle was landscaped by Capability Brown, and the park, woods and lakes are home to a wide variety of birds. After the death of Lady Baillie the castle was bequeathed to the nation and is managed by the Leeds Castle Foundation, a registered charity. The Park is open throughout the year, from 10am till 5pm in summer and slightly shorter hours in the winter. Enquires: phone 01622 7654000

Leeds village

The church of St Nicholas had Anglo Saxon origins with a narrow and high nave, and from the north aisle it is possible to see two Anglo Saxon windows above the north arcade. The massive early Norman tower is built of ragstone, but the corners of the tower and surrounds to the tower windows are of tufa, a rock which forms on the beds of streams in limestone areas. On top of the tower is the small spire, removed as it became unsafe in the 1930s but replaced in 1963. The site of an Augustinian Priory is a few hundred metres to the south of the church.

North Downs Way

One of the ten National Trails, this long distance route extends 150 miles from Farnham to Dover, with an alternative route to Canterbury. The path splits at Broughton and the alternative routes go through Wye or Canterbury, but both end up in Dover. Part of the route follows the top of the North Downs ridge, and in Kent, the path is located in the Kent Downs Area of Outstanding Natural Beauty.

The walk to Leeds

Walk along the right side of All Saints church (1) and on to the surfaced path across a field to reach the B2163 by the school. Turn right, noting the granite war memorial, and pass beneath the railway bridge and the sign to Hollingbourne station – and then the impressive old half timbered Godfrey House on left, built 1587 and restored in the 19th century. Where the road bends right (this is Eyhorne Street – which is the name both of the village and the street), go left along what looks like (and is) a driveway to Grove Mill Cottage.

Once beyond where the drive bends right, to the last house on the right, with its Private sign, and just before reaching the gate and stile, turn right on the path by a hedge of coniferous trees. This leads through to a path between the trees and a wire fence bordering an open field. Turn left over a stile and the path immediately divides but we follow the hedge on the left. Keep straight ahead over another stile, with a hedge on the left, and looking over to the right you will see the footbridge across the motorway, which you will be crossing later in this walk. Keep going past another stile and this leads on towards the wood, Coombe Wood, which is on the left. In the corner of the field, a stile will lead on to a track through the woods. This track emerges on to the narrow Hospital Road (2), and we turn right here, passing Warren Wood Cottage, then beneath the motorway and out on to the A20.

Turn left alongside the noisy A20, and where the main road bends left, turn right, following the signpost to Broomfield. Take care crossing this road, and doing so before the corner gives more chances of survival. After about 30 metres alongside this minor road, turn right into Leeds Castle Park at the welcome notice and im-

Leeds Castle

mediately left of the green on the golf course, bearing slightly left, to reach the main driveway. Turn right and follow this to the lake, with the ducks, white and black swans, and other waterbirds. Turn right towards the castle and at the main entrance turn left, still following the drive (3). This soon splits and we take the left fork, alongside a lake, and walk past the Upper car park and a cattle grid to walk on to the narrow drive. When this bends left, fork right across the grass at a yellow tipped post with a Len Valley sign and follow the line of posts to a kissing gate at the right-hand side of the cricket field.

Walk alongside the cricket pitch, through a kissing gate and across another field towards the right of a house and a massive, modernised clapboard barn. Cross straight over the narrow road, with the magnificent old Battel House on the left. This is an early 14th-century stone building and its plan is in three sections, like a half-H design. Nearly 100m along to the right, are the five Battel Hall Cottages, early 17th-century buildings, timber-framed with brick nogging. Go straight on across the field and through two kissing gates to reach St Nicholas church (4), a stone building with a squat

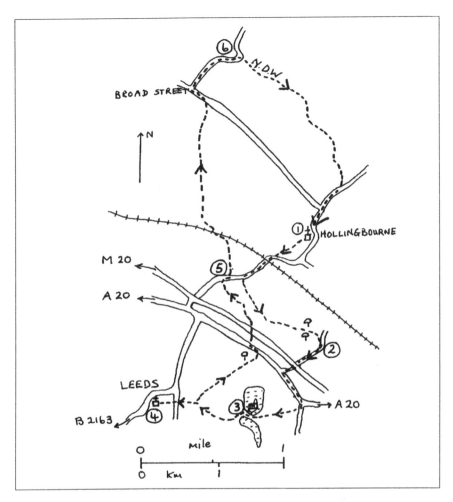

tower and pinnacle spire above it. Inside the church is a memorial to Lady Baillie, who restored Leeds Castle in the 1930s. The village of Leeds is along the road to the left.

Retrace steps to the far side of the cricket field and then fork left, alongside the fence, and enjoy the wonderful views of the castle, with the North Downs scarp in the distance, but try to ignore the view of the M20. At the end of the fence, go right, down to a stile by the gate, and on to the surfaced walkway and straight ahead between two lakes and then the path between trees. Cross the next driveway, pass through a beech plantation, planted in 1990 to replace some of the trees lost in 1987, and across the golf course back to the main road. There was a peacock strutting along the fairway when I last walked this section.

Cross over the road and turn left, to walk along until reaching a track between trees leading to the right, and over the M20 by means of a footbridge. Once over the bridge, turn left along the field margin at first, and then head diagonally across the field towards a small stile in the hedge. Over the stile and a few metres to the right is another stile to get out of this field and on to a stony track. Turn left and follow this track down to the farm, passing between the pond on the right and the buildings on the left, and reach the surfaced driveway. Walk on past the Hollingbourne Village Hall to reach the village street by the Windmill pub.

Turn right along this road (5), passing the village shop on the left and Post Office on the right, and the left turn for the longer route via the North Downs. However for the short way to Hollingbourne church, keep ahead through the village, to pass beneath the railway bridge, and then just before the school, by the War Memorial, turn left to take the path across the fields to Hollingbourne church.

Hollingbourne to the North Downs Way

From the church (1), take the surfaced path across the field to Eyhorne Street, as described in the Leeds Walk. Ignore the left turn followed for the walk to Leeds and continue a little further into the village, looking for the path (5) to the right. Turn here to pass between buildings along a driveway which narrows to a path between gardens. Reach a stile and, beyond this, go diagonally left across the field, to a gap in the hedge. Keep straight on across the next field to a stile and a green drive. Turn left for a few metres (with the railway station to the right) and reach a field. After a further 30 metres, turn right, over the railway line, taking heed of the impeccable advice "Stop, Look and Listen". Old iron kissing gates are on both sides of the railway.

Once across the line the path splits, and we turn left to walk alongside the hedge and railway to the bottom of the field. Cross a stream and head diagonally right across the middle of the next field, to the corner of a patch of mixed deciduous woodland. From here cross an open field to the edge of more woodland, when a white house at the foot of the Downs is straight ahead. We are on the edge of a very large field, like a stretch of prairie (except for the patches of woodland all around – which include a few willow indicating that we are on the clay with its damp patches), and marker posts show the route. The path splits and either route will take us to Broad Street seen ahead. At the road, turn left along what is part of the ancient trackway called Pilgrims Way.

Where a narrow road turns right towards Hucking, this is our route, to take us up the steep slope of the scarp. The road is deeply sunken in places and the banks have a wealth of wild flowers, some of which are still showing colour, though the wild strawberries which cover the bank in places, are long since over. There is still ragwort, and pink campion and herb robert, as well as blackberries.

Where the road bends left, we turn right on to the North Downs Way (6), by going up a few steps to emerge into the open, with wonderful views down to Broad Street and the plain beyond. Follow this path, with shrubs on left and grassy patch on right, with grazing land sloping down to the plain where the flat land is cultivated for crops.

We walk along the top of the scarp and reach a stile, then pass through a small Woodland Trust wood down a few steps. At a T-junction with a stony path turn left for a few metres, before turning right to continue along the North Downs Way, in woodland, though with open fields a few metres to the left. Emerge from the woods and pass beneath the electricity wires, keeping straight ahead on a grassy path between shrubs and undergrowth. Reach a wooden kissing gate, where more wonderful views open up, and you can work out where you were walking half an hour ago. Admire the old oast house down to the left, and beyond it, in the trees, is Hollingbourne.

The scarp ahead is quite scalloped with steep little valleys or coombes, and we reach a field margin then walk along a grassy track between wire fences, where pheasants may be seen and heard. Go on through the kissing gate by the large wooden gate, and emerge on to open grassland, where we begin to descend, towards grass and gorse. At the next wooden gate, with kissing gate, go right and descend more steeply, across a grassy slope and heading directly towards the imposing church tower. Looking around the landscape from this point it is difficult to imagine there are motorways nearby, and this is a well-peopled area. It is so idyllic.

Reach another kissing gate by a large gate, and walk along the field margin with a hedge on the left, and the road steeply down below. Continue down to the road and the village, emerging very close to the Dirty Habit, a Free House – situated on the Pilgrims Way.

Walk on past the wonderful old house next door to the pub, and then a few cottages, before reaching the magnificent Hollingbourne Manor; and then the church, with the Vicarage opposite.

Longer walk

If planning to combine the two walks, follow the instructions given above for the Leeds walk as far as point 5, and then move to point 5 in the instructions for the Hollingbourne walk (except for the fact that you will need to turn left and not right, as written above).

Pheasants: seen and heard on this walk

October

Reculver

These flat walks pass wetland areas and canals but most of the land is farmed for crops and at this time of year much farming activity may be noticed. The only small hills seen are topped by windmills or churches, and the large sea wall is the highest feature in the northern part of the walk.

Distances: The walk from Reculver is just over 8 miles and the walk from St Nicholas at Wade is 5½ miles. They can be linked together to give a longer walk of 10 miles.

Time required: 4-5 hours for the longest walk.

Terrain: very flat though likely to be damp, or worse.

Maps: Landranger 179 or Explorer 150, Canterbury and the Isle of Thanet.

Starting point: Reculver Country Park, GR226692. This is reached along the minor road leading from the A299 3 miles east of Herne Bay. The alternative starting point is at St Nicholas at Wade, just off the A28 and A299, GR265668.

Amenities: refreshments are available at Reculver and at pubs passed on the route, in Sarre and St Nicholas at Wade. Herne Bay is the nearest town and is accessible by bus and train. The town contains a Tourist Information Centre (01227 361911)

The Month

Weather

The month often has an early taste of winter, but occasionally brings back thoughts of sunny summery days too, if a settled anticyclonic spell dominates the weather for a few days. However there is generally a wet and windy spell, brought by Atlantic depressions and this year (1998), a series of deep depressions brought periods of strong winds with several very wet days. Average rainfall for October is about 70mm, though in 1939 a total of 350mm fell in places. It is not just the recent (and possibly exaggerated) talk of Global Warming that has caused large variations of climate. Temperatures were generally mild, with daily maxima often up to 18° or 19°, and in mid-month sunny days occurred, though not as a prolonged spell, merely the result of small ridges of high pressure in between the succession of depressions. Rainy days, though numerous, were not very wet, unlike in parts of western and northern England, where a very wet month was experienced, with severe flooding in the Midlands and Wales.

The flat and open landscape around Reculver and the Isle of Thanet is a windy location and in the windy weather of this month was especially so. The only good thought about the strong winds which blew over the former marshland was that they mainly came from a westerly direction, which is milder than the bitterly cold easterlies which can blow here in the winter.

"Much rain in October, much wind in December"
We shall see.

The Countryside

This is a month of great activity in the bird world, with migrants coming and going, to find a climate and conditions to suit their taste for the winter. Our summer visitors are on the move though many

Geese in flight

may still be seen early in the month, – e.g. late warblers, flycatcher, wheatears, swallows and house martins. These will have all departed by the end of the month, as they go south for warmer conditions. Arriving from the north and east are those birds which come here for the warmth, as the land in their breeding grounds in Scandinavia and the Arctic becomes frozen solid. Brent geese will be arriving early in the month, especially if there is a spell of easterly or northerly weather, and by the end of the month all the winter visitors will be flooding in. Thrushes, waders, geese, and ducks, may be in fields, near the sea, on the shore, or on the patches of shingle, as there are suitable habitats for all varieties of birds. Many birds, not only the migrants, join together in flocks, especially the finches and the starlings. Why do they flock together? Warmth, security and food have been suggested, but there seem flaws in this reasoning. Food would have to be shared out amongst more beaks. Security would attract all the predators. Perhaps they just like being together?

On the walk, we are likely to see lapwings showing off their aerobatics, and moorhens will be skulking around the areas of water. Herons too are common in this watery environment, and we can admire their leisurely flight as they pass overhead with no apparent effort.

Hedges and some of the trees are looking quite dramatic with their prolific fruits and berries. Horse chestnuts drop their conkers, to be gathered up and stored by grey squirrels. These trees also start to drop their leaves, as they are amongst the first trees to do so. On the twigs, the leaf scars can be

Conkers

seen, and it is these horseshoe shaped scars which gave the tree its name. Fungi too are numerous – especially in a wet year such as this one (1998).

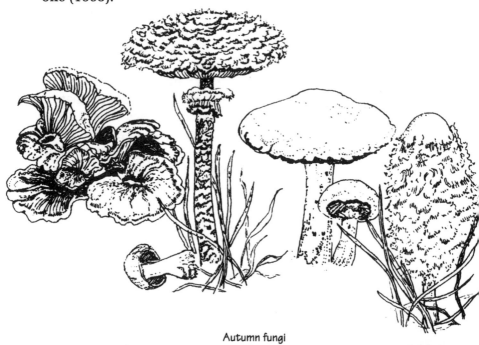

Autumn fungi

Along the Way

Reculver

This is the site of the Roman fort of Regulbium, one of a chain built by the Romans to protect the Wantsum channel, and dating from AD250. The walls are of Kentish rag, with a rubble core, and are about 2.4m (8ft) thick, and formerly just over 6m (20ft) high. Adjacent to it is the site of the Saxon St Mary's Abbey, built by Augustine in the 7th century, and often noted as a landmark for sailors coming up the Thames Estuary. Tradition says that Ethelbert was converted to Christianity here in the 7th century. Reculver was partially eroded by the sea in the 18th century, and because of erosion the old church was abandoned. It is now a ruin, and the new church of St Mary was built at Hillborough in1876. Coastal erosion was largely stopped about 1810, after the sea defences had been built.

Reculver coast

This stretch of coastline is a very important area in the summer months for birds, flowers and butterflies, and notable amongst the summer visitors are the sand martins which nest in cliffs along the coast. Wintertime is also special for birds, and in spring and autumn an amazing number of migratory birds can be seen.

Parts of the cliffs are of sediment about 55 million years in age, and noted for their fossils, which have been exposed by erosion. Sea defences have been protecting the coast for nearly 200 years, but there is still some erosion of the cliffs. A large sea wall extends eastwards from Reculver towards Margate, and at New Haven the sea wall bends inland but a shingle ridge keeps straight on. In about 1486, the Archbishop of Canterbury John Morton, had a channel cut to the sea here, from near Sarre. Around here, the birds can make use of the seashore, shingle ridge, lagoon and the former marshland which still has a little wetland but is mainly farmland. The marshland inland is cultivated, but is also good for wildlife, with numerous voles and kestrels all year, and visiting short eared owls and hen harriers in autumn. The reed beds are ideal for nesting birds and dragonflies.

The Canterbury City Council created the 91 acre (37ha) Reculver Country Park, including the Roman fort and the later monastery of Reculver. Dominating the park are the twin towers, remnants of the 12th-century parish church. The church was demolished in 1809 because it was feared the sea would reach it, but Trinity House saved the towers, as a memory and also as a landmark. The Information Centre, at the car park, is only open on Sundays in October, but the cafe at the caravan site is likely to be open on other days.

Saxon Shore Way

The Saxon Shore Way follows the coastline and passes over marshes, sea walls and cliffs, as well as through farmland and woods. It extends from Gravesend to Hastings, a distance of 140 miles, and is rich in Historical Sites and Natural History. For part of its length near Reculver it is followed by the Wantsum Walk, a linear walk of 8 miles from Herne Bay to Birchington, on cliff tops and sea walls.

Sarre

The main road into Thanet came through here until the Thanet Way was built, and it was a major stopping place on this route. It was a port in Roman and early medieval times, and a double tide was experienced. Silting up caused its decline, and the population also declined as a result of the Black Death in 1349. The parish church of St Giles was abandoned in 16th century, and to the east of Sarre is an old windmill, which we pass on the walk.

St Nicholas at Wade

St Nicholas court is an L-shaped 18th-century house, containing underground chambers. Origin is obscure but perhaps connected with Lollards. The village has some imposing houses, and the 17th-century brick gables show Dutch influence. The church of St Nicholas-at-Wade is impressive, and the tower can be seen for miles. It is located at the ford or wading place across the River Wantsum, where the village was established. The original church was built in the 12th century, of flint, ragstone and other local materials, but was remodelled in the 14th and 15th centuries. Amongst the most interesting features inside the church are the arches on the south side of the nave, with dog-tooth carving on the first arch and carved heads on the second. Several memorials to the Bridges family can be seen in Bridges Chapel. Robert Bridges (1844-1930) was Poet Laureate. To the west of the church is the 17th-century Church Cottage, a brick house with double compass end gable.

The Reculver Walk

Start from Reculver (1) from the King Ethelbert Inn and walk back a few metres along the road and when it bends right, turn left along the concrete track towards the caravan site. As the entrance to the site bends left, keep straight ahead along the track, along Saxon Shore Way and Wantsum Way to a gate where the track ends. Turn right alongside a ditch and when the ditch ends keep straight ahead, towards the windmill perched on the hill ahead. Come alongside another ditch and the noise of waders or flocks of finches may be heard, as we reach a footbridge with small stiles at each end. Go on into a large grassy field with a broad ditch on our right where the first of the day's moorhens may be seen – there are likely to be many more in this wetland environment. Pass a small reservoir, resting place for a variety of birds.

Go over a stile at the end of the field and turn right for a few metres, then left along a concrete track, passing beneath the railway line, and climbing a slight hill, a rarity on this walk, to reach a narrow road (2). Here is Chislet Mill, with only the tower remaining. It is of corrugated iron, and is the remains of a Kentish smock mill, wrecked by a sudden squall in 1916. There had probably been several earlier mills on this site, but this one dates from 1765.

Down to our left is Roman Galley, a pub built for drivers on the A299 Thanet Way, and we keep straight ahead, over this road, which dates from 1934. At the T-junction turn right, signposted London, but when this road bends right to join the main London road, we turn left along the narrow road. When this bends right, turn left along a driveway for a few metres and just before reaching the garden, go right through an iron gate alongside a ditch on the right mar-

Reculver ruins

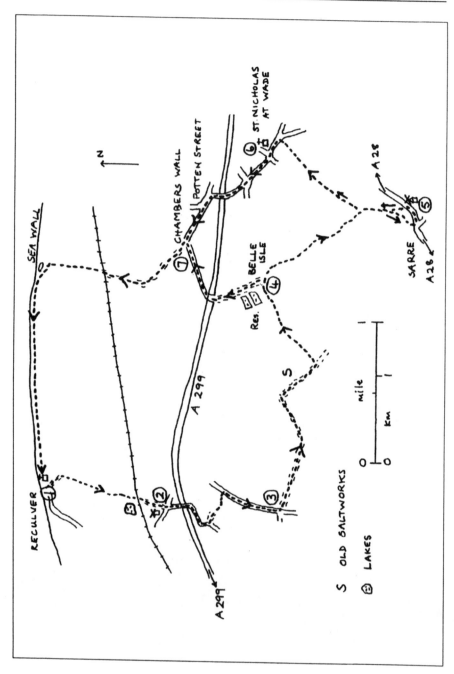

gin of a paddock. Pass a stile at the end of this field and walk on along the driveway which leads through to a road.

Turn right here to pass some old cottages and then alongside the ditch, North Stream. Pass a pub on the right and then Keel Farm, also on the right. Where the small road goes right, we turn left (3), through an iron gate and along a stony track between a ditch and a fence heading out across the reclaimed marshland. This route is Snake Drove, one of the drove roads used to provide access to the marshes from 13th century or earlier. Slightly elevated, as are all the tracks around here, and bordered by reeds in the ditches or by hedges, the droves are wildlife refuges, and shelter for small birds. Long views open up across the flat landscape, often with little tractors buzzing around, as this is a time of great activity on the farmland. Over to the left, on its elevated causeway can be seen the traffic of Thanet Way and in the far left are the towers of the ruined church at Reculver.

After half a mile, the track divides and we fork left, still following Wantsum Walk, and after a further quarter mile reach a T-junction. Turn right here on a Permissive Path along Whitfield Sewer (sewer = a drainage dyke), and notice the mounds in the fields to the left. These are the remnants of medieval salt workings, gradually fading into the general landscape as they are repeatedly ploughed. Pass two small footbridges over Whitfield Sewer and just beyond the second, as the track bends slightly right, we turn left on a very straight track alongside a ditch lined by a row of hawthorns. Reach a concrete farm bridge over the River Wantsum, and just keep going along the concrete track which will lead us across the fields, to pass a reservoir (with more water birds) on the left and then reach Belle Isle (4).

Once past the buildings of Belle Island the track splits into three and we turn left along the track leading to Wagtail Farm and the main road A299. Take the bridge over this road and follow the narrow road for half a mile, passing Warehorn to reach Chambers Wall, which is the name of an embankment built in the Middle Ages to protect St Nicholas at Wade, and also the name of a manor house. At this point (7) we are joined by the walk from St Nicholas at Wade, but we turn left off the narrow road, to follow a tarmac track between fields. The track is slightly elevated here, above field level, and field boundaries are ditches and lines of reeds – in this reclaimed landscape.

If it is windy, which is quite likely, a line of hedges will provide noticeable shelter. The first line of hedges is prolific with fruits and berries, and is very popular with birds. The track doglegs, and bends to the right, at a car park where fishermen, dogwalkers and birders may be encountered. The track continues, stony now and not surfaced. Follow the track northwards as it reaches and crosses the railway line by means of two stiles. The railway line is generally on an embankment, and is often bordered by hedges including hawthorn, blackthorn, elderberry, and apples (the last possibly because of cores thrown through train windows).

At the railway line is a choice of routes, either turn left and head straight towards the twin towers, or, slightly longer but recommended for interest, straight ahead, with a large channel alongside to the left. This is the former Wantsum channel, just a drainage dyke now, and fresh water escapes through a channel beneath the sea wall. The Wantsum channel once separated the Isle of Thanet from Kent, and the channel was up to a kilometre in width in places during Roman times. It silted up, and was finally closed when the sea wall was built.

At the sea wall we turn left, but first look at the Information Board for Coldharbour. The sea wall bends inland here, but the shingle ridge continues as a straight line, helping to create a salty lagoon between the shingle and the sea wall. Salt marsh plants enjoy the lagoon environment, as do many wading birds. Ringed plovers and terns nest on the shingle ridge, which is also used as a high tide resting place for many birds.

The sea wall here is called the Northern Sea Wall and was completed in 1808, though there had been earlier sea defences. We just walk along this wall to return to Reculver, noticing a variety of birds, with waders to our right, on the shore, and flocks of finches such as linnets and house sparrows on the left. These flocks can make use of the bushes and rough grass on the left, grasses and seed bearing plants on the shingle at the top of the beach, but can also go into the farm fields, which may have stubble. Flowers grow on the shingle to the right and also on grasses on the bank sloping down from the sea wall. Redshanks, turnstones, cormorants, and numerous gulls are likely to be seen and heard, possibly with pipits and migrating wheatears. Just before the end of the walk pass the ponds of the Lobster Farm on the left. For the grand finale of this walk, I hope you will be as lucky as I was – for, the last time I walked this way, I was treated to the sight of a kingfisher, flashing away down the channel as I approached the caravan site (1).

Walk from St Nicholas at Wade

Start from the church (6) and head north-westwards out of the village. Just beyond the church is Shuart Lane and then the old Church Cottages, as we keep straight ahead to leave the village, and cross over Thanet Way. At the T-junction, turn left to pass through Potten Street, which is on an ancient route across the marshland. Reach Chambers Wall (7), where the walk from Reculver comes in from the left. We fork left here to follow the narrow road and once across the A299 follow the track parallel to the main road but soon turn right to head southwards. This track leads us past Wagtail Farm and between fields, with two small lakes to our right, and on to the crossing point of tracks at Belle Isle (4).

This is where the walk from Reculver comes in from the right, but we keep straight ahead along Wantsum Walk, a bridleway which has a hedge to the right. This goes alongside the small meandering Wade Marsh Stream in a south-easterly direction. Pass an old brick bridge which goes right, but keep straight ahead towards the buildings of Down Barton. Our route takes us on the right side of these, with a slight left bend then right again to pass through an old farmyard and a caravan graveyard, to emerge on to the edge of another field. Keep straight ahead to reach a hedge and walk along the left side of this until reaching a cross-paths. Turn right here, although later our onward route is going to the left here up the field and towards the village of St Nicholas at Wade.

Go through an old iron kissing gate and along a path between hedges, and when this leads to an open field, the windmill of Sarre is straight ahead. Walk along the narrow surfaced path through a field and note the left turn goes off to the windmill, but keep straight on. To the left of the hedge is a hollow with brick huts and then a few houses, as we walk between hedges with sloe berries and reach another kissing gate and go through to the road. The name of the house on the left, Chalk Pit Cottage, explains the origin of the deep hollow. Chalk was quarried here in medieval times to use for marling the fields on reclaimed marshes. At the road turn left, and pass a bus shelter with seats (may be welcome) and then the Crown Inn on the right, before reaching the windmill (5).

Turn left off the road, opposite the windmill and after a short path with the old quarry down to the left, turn right along the path followed earlier and retrace steps to the hedged path and the iron kissing gate and the cross-paths. From here, go straight ahead, north-east up the gentle hill towards the church tower in St Nicholas at Wade.

The narrow tarmac path leads through the fields up a gentle hill and once on the level, the village can be seen. Reach a road on the left and a few houses, but keep straight ahead, and along the margin of a playing field before reaching the road. Turn left, and soon left again, to walk through the village, passing between The Sun and The Bell, to reach the flint faced church with its prominent tower (6).

The longer walk

To combine the two walks, follow the Reculver walk from points 1-4, as far as Belle Island, and then join on the St Nicholas at Wade walk from points 4-6, which is the end of that walk. Then follow the instructions from the beginning of the St Nicholas walk, as far as point number 7, from which point the Reculver walk is followed to the end (1).

November

Lullingstone, Shoreham, Darent Valley

Less than ten miles from the urban sprawl of London, and quite close to the drone of the M25, urban life can be forgotten as this rural walk takes you around the gentle hills of Lullingstone Park and down by the riverside.

Distance: 8½ miles

Time required: 4 hours

Terrain: flat near the river but otherwise undulating. Several small stiles – and one giant. There are short walks suitable for wheel chairs starting from the Visitor Centre.

Maps: OS Landranger 177 or Explorer Maps 147 and 162

Starting point: Lullingstone Visitor Centre (phone 01322 865995) at King-fisher Bridge, GR526638. The centre is open every day of the year, except Christmas Day, 11-5 in summer and 11-4 in winter. Bus and train from Sevenoaks, and London. There are railway stations at Shoreham and Eynsford.

Amenities: small café at the visitor centre; pubs in Shoreham. Nearest towns are Orpington and Swanley and there is a Tourist Information Centre at Rochester (01634 843666)

The Month

Weather

November is really an autumnal month, although occasional snatches of winter may be revealed with cold snaps from the north. Unsettled westerly weather often dominates however, and rain and winds are frequent, as depressions pass over and blow away the last of the autumnal leaves. Strong winds occur in association with the westerlies, but occasional strong winds may blow from the east and they are generally cold. The famous so-called 'Protestant wind' of November 1688 blew the ships of William of Orange from Holland to Torbay. He had hoped to land at Bexhill! November is often the wettest month of the year, although occasional calm spells bring the mists and fogs for which the month is famous. The Channel is still averaging about 14°C and is a source of warmth. Kent in 1998 was a drier than average month with sunshine totals well above average, the first and third weeks being especially fortunate. The daily maxima temperatures were well above 10°C until mid-month, when 9°C or less was recorded. A cold spell from 20th-24th was the result of a short burst of Siberian weather, which is much more usual and frequent in January or February. Pessimists assumed that the winter would be very harsh (time will tell) but past records show that a cold spell in November is not necessarily followed by a cold winter. The old weather saying: *"Flowers in bloom late in autumn indicate a bad winter"* is also slightly pessimistic but is an indication of the weather that has gone, rather than a prediction of the future.

The Countryside

Early in the month a few remnants of autumnal colours may be seen, but by mid-month the trees have lost their leaves and the hedgerows are bare. Old birds' nests are clearly seen, and for local people it is amazing how many nests were never noticed last summer. Fruits and berries may still be surviving unless already eaten by the hungry birds and animals, with winter visiting thrushes, the redwing and fieldfare, having joined the local thrushes and blackbirds to devour the holly and hawthorn. In times of shortage, they even move on the pyracantha and cotoneaster in gardens. Bird life is often scarcer than in the summer months, except when large flocks are encountered, as many types of birds group together in large numbers in winter. Why they should do this may seem rather strange, when they are all competing for limited supplies of food, and birds are not noted for sharing (see comment on page 107). Just before dusk, groups of birds can be seen heading off to their regular roosting places – a very attractive sight on a clear calm evening, just after the sun has sunk below the horizon.

Most of the ploughing has now been completed and many fields of winter cereals are already showing a couple of inches of green growth. There are also green patches on field margins and verges, brightening up the generally brownish appearance of parts of the

Holly and berries

countryside. Work on the farms will include tidying hedges and clearing out ditches in the clay lands in the county. Muck spreading is another seasonal activity in the fields of grassland, many of which still exist in this area. Cattle as well as horses may be seen in many fields, and the horses may be sporting their winter coats, especially in a wet spell of weather.

Along the Way

Lullingstone

The Country Park extends over 215 hectares (535 acres) of downland and woodland and is crossed by many footpaths. It was originally a medieval deer park, and there were 200-300 deer here until World War II. The chalk areas are rich in flowers and the woodlands contain a variety of trees, including some ancient oaks, up to

Pollarded oak trees

Lullingstone Castle

700 years old. Pollarded trees and areas of open woodland contribute to the creation of a wide range of habitat for wild life. There is now a popular golf course. The Visitor Centre at Kingfisher Bridge was opened in April 1991 and has been recently refurbished and extended.

The 18th-century Queen Anne style house is called Lullingstone Castle, and is an historic family mansion, built round an earlier Tudor building. It was visited by Henry VIII and Queen Anne, and is now owned by the Hartdyke family. St Botolph church is of flint and brick, and dates from the early 14th century, though looks Norman. It can be visited at all times. The gatehouse is 16th century, built of red brick and three storeys in height. The terracotta panels on the turrets, with quatrefoil loops, are all for decoration and not for defence. Until the mid-18th century, there was a second, inner gatehouse

The castle, church and gatehouse sit on three sides of a large lawn. The castle is open to visitors from April to September, but only at weekends and Bank Holidays

Lullingstone Roman Villa

This has been scientifically excavated, and is the best preserved of several Roman buildings found in the Darent valley. An audio tour explains the lifestyle of the owners of this luxurious villa. The villa dates from AD80-90, and reveals signs of domestic comfort with bathhouses and underfloor heating. There are also well-preserved mosaics to be seen, as well as displays with a variety of relics from Roman times. It is an English Heritage site, and opening times are from 10am-4pm November to March, but 10am-6pm the rest of the year. Special events for making mosaics and pottery are occasionally arranged (phone 01304 612013).

Darent Valley Walk

The river Darent flows from the greensand ridge, northwards across the marshes into the Thames. Over-extraction of water has caused the river to shrink and nearly disappear in prolonged dry spells, but the River Authority is now working to solve many of the problems as well as to enhance the countryside along the river. The Darent Valley Path extends from Sevenoaks to Dartford, passing through Otford, Shoreham and Eynsford.

Shoreham

This small village has an attractive range of housing styles. William Blake (1757-1827) stayed at Water House for a time, and this house later became the home of Samuel Palmer (1805-1884) who painted many of his landscapes whilst living here. There is still a School of Art in the village. The church of St Peter and St Paul dates from the 12th century, with part of the west wall and adjoining nave arch being original from that time. A path from the lych gate through the churchyard is lined with yew trees planted in 1867. The entrance to the church is through the 15th-century porch, formed from the large root of an oak tree. Of the several interesting features inside, perhaps most outstanding is the pre-Reformation rood screen. Other features include the large painting on the west wall, and the Burne-Jones window on the south wall. This was the only window to survive the bombing in World War II. It portrays Joy, Creation and Love, and was a memorial to Sir Joseph Prestwich (1812-96) a famous geologist, who lived in the village. The Mildmay chapel was formerly the pew of the Mildmay family, who were responsible for planting the yews in the churchyard and paving the church walk.

Up on the hillside to the west of the village is a chalk cross, memorial to the dead of World War I. There is parking available in Shoreham and several good eating places.

The Walk

From the Visitor Centre (1) follow the sign 1km to Lullingstone Castle and 1km to Roman Villa along the gravelled path beside the river and alongside the lake. This is part of the Darent Valley path, a 15-mile footpath from Dartford to Sevenoaks – marked on signposts by a letter D.

Just before reaching the Roman Villa, our onward route goes up the stepped path on the left, but perhaps you will wish to visit the villa. After your visit, retrace steps a few metres, to the stepped path, and go into the woods, over a stile and on up the hill steadily. Just before the top of the hill, a path goes off to the right, which we ignore apart from admiring the views to the church spire in Eynsford and the viaduct on which you might catch a glimpse of Eurostar. The path ahead soon splits and the left fork goes through a few trees and out on to an open field, to pass to the left of a lone tree. This path leads on to the golf course and towards the Club House, but it is probably better to keep on the straight ahead route along the bracing hill top with no fear of flying golf balls.

Keep straight ahead along a path between two fields, with a large open field to the right. There are several lines of wind break trees on this fairly exposed plateau, but views are quite extensive, over Eynsford to the right and down to Lullingstone castle and the golf course to the left. At the end of the field is a T-junction of paths where we turn left, along the field boundary. Like most of the fields in this area, the soil is very stony. Walk alongside a line of poplars to a stile and keep straight ahead to reach a track, which leads past a field and then paddocks. The buildings and stables of Parkgate Farm are on our left, and the stony track takes us through to a narrow road just beyond where path number 202 goes right through a gate. Our path is number 206, and we turn left at the narrow road, into the car park (2) of the golf course, and turn immediately right across to the far corner of the parking area, where there is a map of Lullingstone Park.

Go through the gate along the surfaced track, with a picnic area to the right, and the club house and a fairway to the left. After 200 metres turn right, following the finger post, pointing to the circular walk on path number 206. Pass between a tee on the right and a

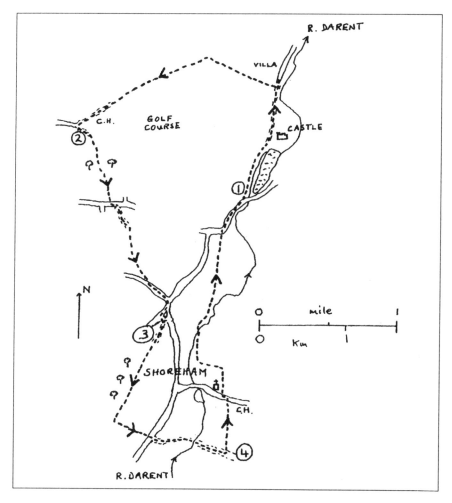

green on the left, and enter the woods, going downhill through beech trees, where bluebells look magnificent in the spring. At the bottom of the slope, cross over a fairway in a dry valley, and up the other side on a broad grassy path between trees. At the top of the slope and the edge of the woods, turn left for about 30 metres to a crossing point of paths. Turn right here, on a bearing of 206, and go through the tall iron gate, by the tall iron stile. This giant is said to be the tallest stile in Kent and was placed there to provide a way over the deer fence which used to exist here.

The narrow path leads between buildings on the left and hedge on the right to reach a stile, then along the margin of the field, to another stile and down a few steps out to the road. Turn left for 100 metres and then go right at a footpath sign, along a stony drive to Homewood Farm, to walk past an isolated house and out to a field, following the path along the right margin. Go over a stile and diagonally down a sloping grassy field, and over another stile on to the narrow Cockerhurst Road, where we turn left, going downhill.

At the T-junction turn right, then bear right at the small grassy island, signposted to Halstead, and after nearly 100 metres turn left just before Darenth Hulme Cottage and Darenth House. The track splits immediately (3), and we take the right fork, and after 30m bend right, on a broad and nearly horizontal path (SR20) along the edge of the woods, with wonderful views down to the left. At the Meenfield Wood sign, do not fork right but just keep straight ahead along the woodland margin. This is the Terraced Walk and was constructed as a gallop for horses. It passes just above the Shoreham Cross, and through areas of recent planting. At the point, where a path turns left, there is a particularly good view over Shoreham, but we keep straight ahead and reach an area where there is woodland on our left as well as right. At the end of the wood, the path splits, and we turn left and go downhill on a path (SR9) which becomes a track to reach Filston Lane, to the left of the oast house.

Cross straight over the narrow road and continue along Water Lane passing Kennel Cottage and along the path. Robin Wood is on the left, a memorial to a former resident of Kennel Cottage. Go on over a footbridge (with Peter's Bridge in the concrete), and cross the Darent by an old mill and oast house and go on up the hill. Cross part of the golf course and just before reaching the railway line, turn left (4), following the Darent Valley Path. This path leads on to the cricket field and straight on through a black iron gate, passing more of the golf course and reaching the road to the left of the Club House. Our route goes left here, but a few yards up to the right is the railway station, with the small Shoreham Countryside Centre containing exhibits and reference material on local geology, history and wild life. Certain items are on sale, though it is only open Saturdays, Sundays and Bank Holidays 2.30-5.30, from April till the end of October.

The porch of Shoreham church

Turn left to walk towards the village, but just before the first house (The Vicarage) turn right along the Darent Valley Path, along the field margin. A gate will enable you to visit the church and village if you wish – it is well worthwhile – and it is possible to link up with the path from the other end of the main street in the village. However, the route is along the field margin, and at the end of this large field, turn left, and go over a couple of stiles to the river. Cross the footbridge and follow the yellow arrow and yellow D to take the Darent Valley Path along the riverside.

If you turn left through the kissing gate and into the churchyard you can admire the view along the line of yew trees, with the hillside in the background where you were walking an hour or so ago. After visiting the church continue through the village and walk alongside the river to the bridge and the ford. By the ford is a World War I memorial, with the inscription "Remember as you look at the cross on the hill those who gave their lives for their country 1914-1919".

Walking alongside the river leads past Flint Cottage with its decorated front, and then the house where Samuel Palmer lived from 1827-1834/5. An alternative route for the Darent walk goes between the wall of this house and the river, and so just continue along here to join the path which came past the churchyard gate, as described above.

After rejoining the other path, follow the D, and cross three fields and alongside an old hop field, to join the road on a bend. Keep straight ahead along the road, passing the Hop Shop where English dried flowers are available, and then on to the starting point a further 300 metres along the road.

December

Penshurst to Chiddingstone

We are visiting the heart of the Garden of England and the Valley of Eden.
Parkland, woods and fields are all part of this walk, together with two
attractive villages.

Distance: nearly 8 miles

Time required: about 4 hours

Terrain: gentle though muddy in places (unless frozen hard), and stiles are numerous

Maps: O.S. Landranger 188 or Explorer 147

Starting point: Penshurst, at a parking area alongside the B2176 leading northwards from the village centre. GR526439. Penshurst is 4 miles north-west of Tunbridge Wells and can be reached along the B2188 or the B2176. Buses from Tunbridge Wells to Edenbridge pass through Penshurst which also has a railway station close to the route of the walk.

Amenities: Pubs and tea shops in both Penshurst and Chiddingstone. **Nearest town** is Royal Tunbridge Wells, which also has a Tourist Information Centre (01892 515675)

The Month

Weather

This is the first month of winter but temperatures are often more in keeping with the autumn, and an average December will give mild and unsettled weather rather than cold weather. Snowy Christmases are quite rare in this part of the country, though it is certainly not unusual to see some snow during the month. The main source of warmth is not the sun, but the Atlantic Ocean, and in westerly conditions this influence does extend to the south-east corner of England. If the wind direction changes, to blow off the continent or from the north, a marked difference will result.

The north wind doth blow, And we shall have snow,
And what will the robin do then, poor thing.

This rhyme has some accurate meteorology, not that it will snow every time there is a northerly wind, but it is certainly a possibility in the winter months. Temperatures will fall from double figures down to a daytime maximum of only 1° or 2°C, as happened in 1998 at the beginning of the month, though by the second week day maxima were up to a very mild 15°C. This was a changeable month, with rainfall below average, but several dull grey days – typical British weather! This is rather different from some of the harsh December weather of the past, the worst in recent times being 1962-63, when snow and ice took effect on Boxing Day, and not only saw out the year, but did not really disappear for two months.

The Countryside

Parts of the countryside look bleak and bare, but it is by no means a dead time of the year. Many types of birds and animals are not as numerous as in summer, and a few have migrated or gone into hibernation – or even died off, as happens with many insects, but it is still worth looking out for birds and animals. Any which are out and about can often be seen more easily in the bare trees and hedgerows. This is the time when many hedgerows are receiving an annual trim or a more long term cutting and laying. Where left alone there may be long strings or clusters of the whitish old man's beard, especially in the chalklands, with the bright red berries of cuckoo pint at the foot of the hedge, and the red berries of the black or white bryony, two unrelated plants but both having red berries. Other bright red berries can be seen on holly trees and also on the yew trees in church yards, and in other locations too. South-east England is one of the yew's most successful locations. Famous as a suitable wood for making longbows in the Middle Ages, the tree is also noted for its poisonous berries.

A few birds are able to eat the seeds from within the berries, and live, and in recent years another positive feature of the tree is that it has become the source of an anti-cancer drug. Blackbirds, thrushes and greenfinches are birds known to eat the seeds, and with

Yew and berries

other finches and varieties of tits these are some of the commonest birds at this time of year. Flocks of birds (finches, skylarks, gulls, jackdaws) are to be seen in the fields in winter, but much larger flocks are seen on the coasts where mudflats and estuaries are the winter home for millions of geese, ducks and waders. The birds along the coast are fortunate to have such prolific supplies of food, replenished by high tides and then exposed at low tide, twice every 24 hours. These coastal areas are also unlikely to freeze up, even in cold spells. This month is a good time to look at the bark on trees, as a little experience will enable trees to be recognised even when there are no leaves or fruit to make identification easier.

Along the Way

Penshurst

St John the Baptist is a sandstone church, and dates from 1120 or earlier. The tower dates from the 17th century. Features of interest include memorials to Field Marshal Viscount Gort V.C. and Thomas Boleyn, the brother of Anne Boleyn. The Becket window by the south-west door was given by the parishioners for the 800th anniversary of Saint Thomas à Becket, Archbishop of Canterbury, whose last public act was to install Willhelmus (or Willelmus) as first village priest in Penshurst, in 1170. The village contains several other interesting old buildings from 200- 400 years ago, notably the two old half-timbered cottages, joined by a third cottage, beneath which is the entry to the churchyard. Other cottages have half timbered upper parts with ragstone lower, jettied out and rendered. The Rectory is 18th century.

Stone coffin lid with the nun of the Albigensian cross in Penshurst church

Penshurst Place

This magnificent local sandstone Manor House with its famous Barons Hall (said to be the finest of its kind in England), dates from the 14th century though with several later additions. The original house was built in 1340 for Sir John de Pulteney, a wealthy wool merchant, who was Mayor of London. It has been the family home of the Sydneys since 1552, and is now the home of Viscount De L'Isle. The Toy Museum is a notable attraction here, together with the Venture Playground and 4 hectares (10 acres) of gardens, with some original terraces and walls. There is a formal Italian garden. Only open from March to October.

Chiddingstone

Though only a tiny village, it does have a school, church and a shop, and its single street is very photogenic and frequently used by film makers. Part of "Queen Elizabeth" starring Glenda Jackson was filmed here. Much of the village is owned by the National Trust and includes 16th and 17th-century houses of timber with brick or plaster infillings. Particularly impressive and attractive are the Post Office and Castle Inn. The Post Office is mentioned in a deed of 1453 and in 1517 was bought by Sir Thomas Boleyn, father of Anne, and eventually passed into the hands of the Streatfeild family in 1700. The earliest reference to the Castle Inn was in 1666, when it was a private property. Next door to it is an antique shop which was formerly a butcher's. The large wrought iron gates on the roadside adjacent to the Castle are on what used to be the road, but this was diverted by Streatfeild whose home was in the castle, a 19th-century mock Gothic building, built on the site of a 17th-century mansion. He did not want the road to go past his home and whilst diverting the road, he demolished several houses and created the small lake in a landscaped garden. In 1936 the castle was sold by Streatfeild to the Astors, who really only wanted the land for its shooting. Denys Eyre Bower owned it from 1955-1977, and it was then taken over by a Private Trust. It is open Wednesdays-Fridays and Sundays and Bank Holidays during the summer, and contains much of Bower's collection of Stuart memorabilia and Egyptian and Japanese items.

Several buildings in the village, including the Old Rectory, have hung tiles. The local sandstone church of St Mary the Virgin dates from the 13th century, though there were earlier churches on the site. It contains many fine carvings and a Jacobean font, and a collection of hatchments is situated in the South Aisle. In a glass case is a 'Vinegar Bible' one of very few which have survived with the word 'vinegar' printed instead of 'vineyard'. The church was struck by lightning and devastated by fire in July 1624, and it took five years for the repairs to be completed. Outside the church are other features of interest. A sundial above the south door becomes almost concealed by wisteria in the spring. In the corner of the churchyard is a small building which could have been used by gravewatchers.

The National Trust also owns the large lump of sandstone known as the Chiding Stone which stands on an acre of land given by Lord Astor of Hever. Tradition says that nagging wives were brought here to be chided by the village population.

The Chiding Stone

The Walk

Walk along the roadside to the centre of the village (1) and turn left to pass the Rectory on the left, the Leicester Arms (motto – Honi soit qui mal y pense) on our right, and before reaching the gateway to Penshurst Place, turn left into Leicester Square. Pass beneath the remarkable archway which is an old timbered cottage raised on pillars, to walk along the left side of the church of St John. Go through the first of several narrow stiles to emerge in a field of the Penshurst Estate. To the right is a ha-ha, beautiful hedge and the fine buildings of Penshurst Place with its chimneys and towers. At the end of the field, use two V-shaped stiles to cross a drive, but keep straight ahead through the next large field, with its recently planted lines of trees, and the cricket pitch to the right, in a most idyllic setting. At the end of the next field is another of the same type of stile, beyond which we turn right alongside the fence, to skirt round to the left side of the pond in Penshurst Park, where ducks, geese and possibly a heron may be seen.

Beyond the next V stile is another large field of parkland, and we soon bend left to go uphill in an avenue of trees, including oak and sycamore. Go through another stile and continue up a broad grassy slope, with woodland on the left – and noises of pheasants and woodpeckers. You may see a little owl in this area. Level off at the top of the slope, and pass a marker post beyond which the path divides. There is a right turn (footpath number 423), along a broad avenue, but we go just right of straight ahead (path 422). Cross an area of mixed trees, with some recent planting, but also the remnants of an avenue of very old oaks and, to our right, a newer planted woodland. This stretch is fairly level, but we soon descend to a muddy hollow, which can be very wet in winter, though around here is rich in wild flowers in spring and early summer.

Climb quite steeply up the other side, with the established fir trees of Park Plantation on the left and some recent coppicing on the right, and at the level stretch follow the track as it bends left and leads out to the road (2).

Turn left for 20 metres and then sharp right on the single-track road, following a signpost to Chiddingstone. Pass Cinder Hill Farm and an old oast house, and stay on this road for nearly half a mile,

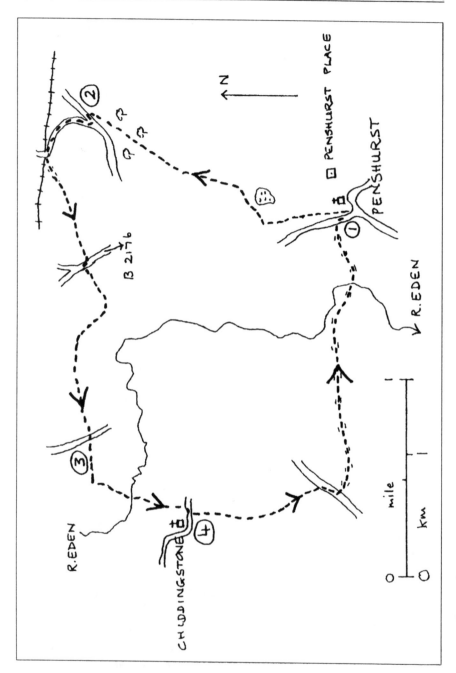

Hop field

and where it turns right to cross the railway line, go straight along the track to Little Moorden. After about 100 metres, fork right off this track, over a stile and along the field margin. At the end of this large field is a cross-paths, but keep straight ahead, alongside an old hop field, with Redleaf Woods on the left. Continue along a track to reach the road at Moorden, a small hamlet with several converted and modernised barns and stables.

Turn right along the road for about 50 metres, and at the second footpath sign turn left through a gate, and after a few metres cross the small stream then walk on, parallel to the stream on our left. Where the path from the other side of the stream comes across to join us, and there are two ways ahead, ignore the left route into a large flattish field, but go through an old gate, uphill, and follow the right margin of the field. At the top corner of this field, go on through a gate and alongside a hop field, and straight on over a stile, with a hedge and hop field to the left. The oast towers of Beckett's Farm are over to the right. Cross a small footbridge and head up the hill towards Sandholes (3).

Pass to the left of the buildings, over a stile and out on to a narrow road. Go straight across and follow the edge of the next two fields, then over a stile and turn left over another stile. Go down the left side of this field, with Somerden Farm across the field to the right. At the bottom of the field is a stile beyond which is a clear path leading to the footbridge over the River Eden. From the river, keep straight ahead and up the slope into Chiddingstone, on a path between fences and then a driveway with houses on the right.

Turn right at the main road (4) and the way ahead is through an iron kissing gate about 25 metres on the left, just before reaching the signpost to the Chiding Stone. Before pressing on, it is worth while to pause and wander around this remarkable interesting village. It is a suitable place for purchasing refreshment or eating your picnic, and women are safe in this village nowadays – but do visit the Chiding Stone to make sure.

Leave the village on footpath 518, go over stiles, across a field and soon come to a larger track. Turn left along this, the Eden Valley Path and follow it through a small wood (The Slips) along a broad and muddy path to the minor road.

Turn right for a few metres along the road, then fork left, walk across a field and turn left to join a track heading eastwards. Where it splits, fork left of the farm buildings at Wat Stock and follow this track back to Penshurst. Easy brisk walking through magnificent countryside, with good views left, to the north. You will see the rather grand Doubleton Farm House across on the slope to the left, as you descend to the bridge over the River Eden. The track comes out on to a surfaced lane, on a bend, but we keep straight ahead over the

river. A notice on a tree mentions Kingfisher Angling and Preservation Society and I looked up and down the river for sight of a kingfisher – but in vain. Just follow the track, and climb slightly up towards the main road, as Penshurst church tower comes into sight. Turn right to return to the starting point.

Kingfisher

Also of Interest:

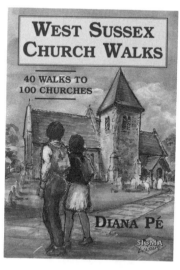

West Sussex Church Walks
Diana Pé

So much more than a walking guide, West Sussex Church Walks contains absorbing histories of the churches featured on each route, plus local history details which enable readers to imagine how people lived in the area up to 1000 years ago. Diana Pé's carefully planned walks range from 3 to 10 miles and cover a variety of terrain from coastal plains and woodland to meandering riversides and gently undulating hills. Fully illustrated with sketch maps and photographs.
£7.95

Best Tea Shop Walks in Surrey & Sussex
Margaret & Barrie Howard

A leisurely walk in the long-neglected countryside of Surrey and Sussex followed by a delicious afternoon tea. "An enjoyable mixture of rambling and relaxation...This book offers a quintessentially English slice of life."
SURREY ADVERTISER
£6.95

Best Pub Walks in Essex
Derek Keeble

Local walker Derek has produced this gem of a book with wonderfully accurate instructions, excellent maps and a wealth of local information.
£6.95

Best Tea Shop Walks in Norfolk
June & Norman Buckley

"*Best Tea Shop Walks in Norfolk* is the perfect companion for those who would like to explore and experience the charms of Norfolk." COMMUNITY NEWS for Halesworth
£6.95

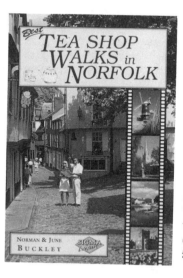

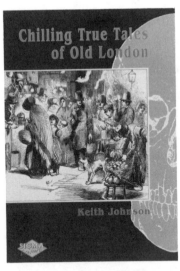